The Black Panther
An anthology

The Black Panther
Black Community News Service
An anthology (1968-1970)

DOBLE J
HISTORY

© Editorial Doble J
C/ Brasil 11, 2º i
41013 Seville, Spain
editorialdoblej@editorialdoblej.com
ISBN: 978-84-96875-57-9

TABLE OF CONTENTS

1. What Was The Black Panther Party?

The Black Panther Party was a progressive political organization that stood in the vanguard of the most powerful movement for social change in America since the Revolution of 1776 and the Civil War: that dynamic episode generally referred to as The Sixties. It is the sole black organization in the entire history of black struggle against slavery and oppression in the United States that was armed and promoted a revolutionary agenda, and it represents the last great thrust by the mass of black people for equality, justice and freedom.

The Party's ideals and activities were so radical, it was at one time assailed by FBI chief J. Edgar Hoover as "the greatest threat to the internal security of the United States." And, despite the demise of the Party, its history and lessons remain so challenging and controversial that established texts and media would erase all reference to the Party from American history.

The Black Panther Party was the manifestation of the vision of Huey P. Newton, the seventh son of a Louisiana family

I

transplanted to Oakland, California. In October of 1966, in the wake of the assassination of black leader Malcolm X and on the heels of the massive black, urban uprising in Watts, California and at the height of the civil rights movement led by Dr. Martin Luther King, Jr., Newton gathered a few of his longtime friends, including Bobby Seale and David Hilliard, and developed a skeletal outline for this organization. It was named, originally, the Black Panther Party for Self Defense. The black panther was used as the symbol because it was a powerful image, one that had been used effectively by the shortlived voting rights group the Lowndes County (Alabama) Freedom Organization. The term "self defense" was employed to distinguish the Party's philosophy from the dominant nonviolent theme of the civil rights movement, and in homage to the civil rights group the Louisiana based Deacons for Defense. These two, symbolic references were, however, where all similarity between the Black Panther Party and other black organizations of the time, the civil rights groups and black power groups, ended.

Immediately, the leadership of the embryonic Party outlined a Ten Point Platform and Program (see the end of this article for full text). This Platform & Program articulated the fundamental wants and needs, and called for a redress of the longstanding grievances, of the black masses in America, still alienated from society and oppressed despite the abolition of slavery at the end of the Civil War. Moreover, this Platform & Program was a manifesto that demanded the express needs be met and oppression of blacks be ended immediately, a demand for the right to self defense, by a revolutionary ideology and by the commitment of the membership of the Black Panther Party to promote its agenda for fundamental change in America.

2. Historical Context of the Founding of The Party

There was no question that the end of the several centuries of the institution of slavery of blacks had not resulted in the assimilation of blacks into American society. Indeed, there was a violent, postemancipation white backlash, manifested in the rise of the Ku Klux Klan, endorsed by the benign neglect of the President and the Congress, codified in the so called Black Codes. The rampant lynching of blacks became a way of life in America, along with the de facto denial to blacks of every civil right, including the rights to vote, to worship, to use public facilities.

From that time forward, then, blacks were obliged to wage fierce survival struggles in America, creating at once the NAACP (National Association for the Advancement of Colored People) to promote integration of blacks into society as full, firstclass citizens and the UNIA (Universal Negro Improvement Association) of Marcus Garvey to promote independence of blacks and eventually a return to Africa. At the same time, there were the effective efforts of former slave Booker T. Washington to establish a separate socioeconomic scheme for blacks. America's response to all such efforts was violent and repressive and unyielding. Thus, despite the mass uprisings by blacks in resistance to the unrelenting violence and the law's delay, despite tacit urgings by blacks to be afforded some means to survive, despite the bold endeavors by blacks to live separate lives in America or leave America, for the next half century, blacks, in the main, found themselves denied of every possible avenue to either establish their own socioeconomic independence or participate fully in the larger society.

Not until nearly 60 years after Plessy was there even the most minimal relief, in the Supreme Court's holding in the 1954 case of Brown v. Board of Education. In Brown, the Supreme Court stated that "separate" was "not equal" for blacks in America (at least with respect to public education). It is noteworthy that Dr. Kenneth Clark (the black psychologist on whose study the Brown court based its findings as to the negative impact on black children of the separate but equal doctrine) noted in 1994 that American schools were more segregated at that time than in 1954, when Brown was decided.

Even after Brown, blacks struggled to integrate and become full partisans in American society, to no avail. From the famous 1955, Montgomery (Alabama) bus boycott to the subsequent voter rights efforts to the dangerous sit ins in all white public facilities led by SNCC (Student Nonviolent Coordinating Committee) workers, the civil rights movement challenged America. Under the spiritual guidance and the nonviolent philosophy of Dr. Martin Luther King, Jr. millions, blacks and whites, protested and marched for freedom and justice for America's black minority, as so many were murdered or maimed for life along the way. Finally, in 1964, the U.S. Congress passed a civil rights act that outlawed racial segregation in public facilities.

It was too little too late. As the images of nonviolent blacks and other civil rights workers and demonstrators being beaten and water hosed by police, spat on and jailed, merely for protesting social injustices shot across America's television screens (a new and compelling phenomenon in American life and popular culture), young urban blacks rejected non-violence. The full expression of this was the violent protest to the brutal police beating of a black man in Watts (Los Angeles), California in the 1965 rebellion that shocked America and set off other such responses to oppression. By 1967, there had been more than 100 major black, urban rebellions in cities across the country. In the same time frame of the same year, 1965, the Vietnam war erupted. As television reports revealed the horrible realities of the war, good American soldiers killing Vietnamese children, America's white youth called the question, and rallied against the war. America's youth, black and white, had become openly hostile to the established order.

3. Rise of The Black Panther Party

It was against this backdrop that Huey P. Newton was organizing the Black Panther Party for self-defense, boldly calling for a complete end to all forms of oppression of blacks and offering revolution as an option. At the same time, the Black Panther Party took the position that black people in America and the Vietnamese people were waging a common struggle, as comrades-in-arms, against a common enemy: the U.S. government. What was most "dangerous" about this was that young blacks, the same urban youth throwing molotov cocktails on America, were listening.

This message was amplified when a small group of Black Panther Party members, led by Bobby Seale, designated chairman of the Party, marched into the California legislature, in May 1967, fully armed. Defined as protest against a pending guncontrol bill (which became the Mulford Act) aimed at the

Party with the position that blacks had a Constitutional right to bear arms, the Party's message that day became a clarion call to young blacks.

When, therefore, in October of 1967, Huey Newton was shot, arrested and charged with the murder of a white Oakland cop, after a gun battle of sorts on the streets of West Oakland that resulted in the death of police officer John Frey, it was indeed the spark that lit a prairie fire. Young whites, angry and disillusioned with America over the Vietnam war, raised their voices with young, urban blacks, to cry in unison: "Free Huey!"

It became a movement of itself, the very embodiment of all the social contradictions, between the haves and have nots, the included and excluded, the alienated and the privileged. The freeing of the black man charged with killing a white cop, the oppressed who resisted oppression, was tantamount to the freedom of everyone.

One result was not only the flowering of the Party itself but a rapid proliferation of other, like minded organizations. Chicanos, or Mexican Americans, in Southern California formed the Brown Berets. Whites in Chicago and environs formed the White Patriot Party. Chinese in the San Francisco Bay Area formed the Red Guard. Puerto Ricans in New York created the Young Lords. Eventually, a group of so called senior citizens organized the Gray Panthers to address the human and civil rights abuses of the elderly in society. The Party expanded from a small Oakland based organization to a national organization, as black youth in 48 states formed chapters of the Party. In addition, Black Panther coalition and support groups began to spring up internationally, in Japan,

China, France, England, Germany, Sweden, in Mozambique, South Africa, Zimbabwe, Uruguay and elsewhere, including, even, in Israel.

At the street level, the Party began to develop a series of social programs to provide needed services to black and poor people, promoting thereby, at the same time, a model for an alternative, more humane social scheme. These programs, of which there came to be more than 35, were eventually referred to as Survival Programs, and were operated by Party members under the slogan "survival pending revolution."

The first such program was the Free Breakfast for Children Program, which spread from being operated at one small Catholic church, in the Fillmore district of San Francisco, to every major city in America where there was a Party chapter. Thousands upon thousands of poor and hungry children were fed free breakfasts every day by the Party under this program. The magnitude and powerful impact of this program was such that the federal government was pressed and shamed into adopting a similar program for public schools across the country, while the FBI assailed the free breakfast program as nothing more than a propaganda tool used by the Party to carry out its "communist" agenda. More insidiously, the FBI denounced the Party itself as a group of communist outlaws bent on overthrowing the U.S. government.

Armed with that definition and all the machinery of the federal government, J. Edgar Hoover directed the FBI to wage a campaign to eliminate the Black Panther Party altogether, commanding the assistance of local police departments to do so. Indeed, as Hoover stated in 1968 that the Party represented "the greatest threat to the internal security of the U.S.," he pledged that 1969 would be the last year of the Party's existence. Indeed, in January of 1969, two Party leaders of the Southern California Chapter, John Huggins and Alprentice "Bunchy" Carter, were murdered at UCLA by FBI paid assassins, with the cooperation of black nationalist Ron Karenga and his US Organization. By the end of that year, nearly every office and other facility of the Black Panther Party had been violently assaulted by police and/or the FBI, culminating, in December, in an FBI orchestrated five hour police assault on the office in Los Angeles and FBI directed Illinois state police assassination of Chicago Party leader Fred Hampton and member Mark Clark.

In the interim, there had been the Oakland police murder of 17 year old Party member Bobby Hutton, in April of 1968; the August 1968 Los Angeles police murder of another 17 year old Panther, Tommy Lewis, along with Robert Lawrence and Steve Bartholomew; numerous arrests, from that of Party chairman Bobby Seale on conspiracy charges in connection with anti-war protests at the 1968 Democratic Convention in Chicago to that of chief of staff David Hilliard on charges of assaulting police officers (in the April 1968 police gun battle in which Bobby Hutton was killed) to a conspiracy to kill the President (Nixon) charge arising from an anti-war speech, to the famous New Haven murder conspiracy case of Bobby Seale and veteran Panther Ericka Huggins. There had been every kind of assault imaginable on the Party's social programs and destruction of Party property. From police raiders who smashed breakfast programs eggs on the floors of churches they invaded to those who crushed Party free clinic supplies underfoot to those who caused the destruction of batches of the Party's newspapers. In addition, intimidation and other such tactics were being employed to undermine the Party's support, to break the spirit and commitment of Party supporters and family members. More sinisterly, perhaps, and subtlety were the activities carried out under the FBI's so called counter-intelligence program known as COINTELPRO, whereby the FBI directed its field offices and local police to destroy the Party through the use of informants, agents provocateur and covert activities involving mayhem and murder.

Nevertheless, the Party survived and continued to build its Survival Programs, which came to include not only the free breakfast programs and free clinics, but also grocery giveaways, the manufacture and distribution of free shoes, school and education programs, senior transport and service programs, free bussing to prisons and prisoner support and legal aid programs, among others.

4. The Free Huey Movement And the Growth of The Party

Hundreds of thousands of black as well as white youth had marched throughout the streets of Oakland and all over America in support of the Free Huey Movement as it had come to be called. While Huey was eventually convicted, it was not on the original charge of first degree murder but for simple manslaughter. Soon, however, even that conviction was set aside and a new trial was ordered. In July of 1970, then, Huey was indeed set free from jail. Thousands greeted him.

The celebrations seemed meaningless in light of the July 7, 1970 murder of 17 year old Jonathan Jackson (George Jacksons brother) in the incident that gave rise to the famous arrest and trial of Angela Davis. The question of Huey's freedom was nearly forgotten when well known Party leader Eldridge Cleaver, living in exile in Algeria, challenged the Party's agenda of social programs and proposed a terrorist one. By the end of 1970, Cleaver was expelled from the Party in a nasty riff that culminated in the murder of Party loyalist Sam Napier in New York. Still, the Party continued to build its programs and move its agenda, as it began to consolidate its efforts in its home base of Oakland, California.

Over the next few years, until 1973, the Party maintained and built its agenda, despite the brutal assassination at San Quentin prison in August of 1971 of Party field marshal and author George Jackson. Nevertheless, in 19723, the Party entered into electoral politics in Oakland by running Bobby Seale and Elaine Brown for public office, for mayor and city councilwoman respectively. Though that election was lost, per se, it allowed the Black Panther Party to solidify a broad base of support for its future efforts. In 1974, there was great upheaval in the internal affairs of the Party, so much so that by the time Huey Newton went into selfimposed exile, rather than stand trial for the murder of a young prostitute (for which he would be acquitted), most of the original leadership was gone. David Hilliard was expelled while in prison; Bobby Seale was expelled. Elaine Brown took over the chairmanship of the Party during those three years that Newton was in exile, in Cuba.

X

5. The Last Chapter

During that time, Brown ran for Oakland public office again, this time garnering more than 44% of the vote along with the support of every labor union in the area. At the next city election, the Party supported and virtually installed Lionel Wilson as mayor of Oakland, the first black to hold that post in the 100 year history of the city. In the meantime, it further solidified its base by fighting for and obtaining funds to build 300 new, replacement housing units for poor people displaced by a local freeway; by entering into a working partnership with certain developers to build up the dilapidated downtown city center in order to provide 10,000 new jobs for Oakland's poor and unemployed. At the same time, a permanent primary school was instituted, which was highly lauded by the California legislature, among others. On Huey's return from exile, then, in 1977, the Black Panther Party was alive and well in Oakland, California, maintaining a strong constituency base in the black and working communities, and prepared to move forward to carry out its primary goal to make Oakland a base for revolution in America.

Soon after Newton's return to Oakland, in July of 1977, however, a combination of the continued, albeit more subtle and sophisticated, activities of the FBI (despite J. Edgar Hoover's death in 1972) and internal stress and conflict came to erode the Black Panther Party. By the end of the decade, it had come to a slow and unheralded demise.

1. Information By Eldridge Cleaver,
Minister of Information, Black Panther Party
(From N. Y. Telephone Interviews with the
Minister of Information). September 28, 1968.
Pages 6, 14

Question: Just who and what are the Black Panthers?

Cleaver: The Black Panther Party is a political party that originated in Oakland, California, and was started by Huey P. Newton, who is the minister of defense of the party, and our chairman, Bobby Seale. The party seeks to organize black people so they can move and take control of the life, the politics, and the destiny of the black community. What really makes the Black Panther Party stand out from other groups that have originated in that community is the fact that we feel it is necessary to use guns in a defensive manner against aggression, particularly by the Police Department, vigilante groups, etc. Because we have used these guns for our defense, this is what most people have come to associate with the Black Panther Party. But this is only one point on our platform. We have a ten-point platform that outlines the basic grievances and the basic desires and needs of black people as we see them, and we seek to organize the people in the black

1

community who have never been organized before, such as the so-called lower class black people who are not candidates for membership in the National Association for the Advancement of Colored People.

QUESTION: Since you have written *Soul On Ice*, and the book has been widely hailed in this country, how do you resolve your relationship now as minister of information for the Black Panther Party and as a social critic?

CLEAVER: I think that the two work very handily together. We're dealing with the same thing, you know. There's no conflict in my book between my politics. The book tries to pass on information, and my position in the party sort of passes on information. We're dealing with interpretations of what we're all involved in, and I see that they work out very well together. As a matter of fact, the book itself has helped considerably in getting a lot of the program and activity of the Panther Party across.

QUESTION: You mentioned earlier that the guns of the Black Panthers are to be used for defensive purposes. We've talked about America as being a violent country. Does not this defensive stand add to this violence?

CLEAVER: Any act of defense could be categorized as violence if there is any type of conflict involved, but I think that some violence or conflict is justified. For instance, I think a man who moves to protect himself from an attack, though he used a violent means to dispel that attack, is completely justified in doing so. The right to self-defense has always been recognized in society, and simply because we have a very violent situation on our hands in this country doesn't mean that we have to forego this particular right.

QUESTION: What are your feelings about the new gun control law? Do you feel that this particular law is geared towards the blacks?

CLEAVER: Yes, I do, particularly here in our local area where we see these vicious politicians who are known to be open enemies of the black community. We see them out in the forefront of the forces calling for gun control. At the same time they're calling for gun control, they're escalating the armament and the preparation of the police department, and supplying them with all kinds of new weapons; and we feel that this is aimed directly at the black community. We live in a time when black people are becoming more and more impatient. The philosophy of non-violence has been murdered along with its prophet Dr. Martin Luther King. The power structure of this country knows that the black liberation struggle is turning to violence as an alternative and so they're moving now to disarm people before anything happens. All of this ballyhoo about gun legislation, we feel, is aimed at disarming the black liberation struggle and the allies of that struggle in the white community.

QUESTION: Would you define the defensive program of the Black Panthers in terms of guns? Do you promote vigilante parties?

CLEAVER: Now, we don't promote vigilante parties, and we don't approve of them. We feel that the primary problem confronting the black people today is the problem of being organized. The chief impediment to organizations of the black community comes from the activities of the police department. The police department functions like an occupying army in the black community, and it intimidates black people. It disturbs meetings, prevents black people from having peaceful assemblies, and the very presence of the police, with the history they have with black people, makes them an undesirable element in our community. We seek to remove them from the community because they are constantly killing and terrorizing our people. We feel that before much more progress can be made, this particular problem has to be dealt with. So we call for the immediate withdrawal of the white racist policemen from our community, and we call for enactment of the principle that those who police our community must live in our community. We want the community to control the policemen who police our communities. We feel that it's a form of community imperialism to have a police force occupying our community that is controlled by the white suburbs. This is an obnoxious situation, and we want it to end.

QUESTION: Have the police department and the Black Panthers ever sat down at the same table and attempted to negotiate any of the problems?

CLEAVER: There have been very minimal direct contacts, such as when we've staged benefits and rallies at auditoriums where security has to be discussed; but they prefer to do that behind closed doors; and they want to meet with us behind closed doors as they've done with a lot of other groups in the black communities. One of the main programs that we should have today is their coming into the communities and putting different groups of black people on these poverty programs and buying them out if they agree to perform in a certain manner. We've been approached by some of the flunkies of the power structure to see if we would be willing to accept some of their Uncle Tom money, but publically they try to pretend that the last thing would do would be to condescend to talk with the Black Panthers. This creates a situation exposing them to a lot of people who feel that public officials and public servants should be open to all elements of the public, and they have an image of being very opposed to everything in the black community, particularly the militants, that speak out.

QUESTION: In a recent issue of *Ramparts* (June 29, 1968), the article about the Black Panthers ("The Persecution And Assassination Of The Black Panthers As Performed By The Oakland Police Under The Direction Of Chief Charles R. Gain, Mayor John Reading, Et Al.") ends with the sentence: "And the chances are, too, that the cops will go on, steadily and inexorably, trying to bust, and if necessary kill, every Panther in Oakland." Mr. Cleaver, what is going to be done to stop police brutality and killing?

CLEAVER: I think that if the people who are standing on the sidelines don't move to harness the police departments of this country (not just in Oakland, because this is something that's going on all over this country), there will be no alternative to the black community but to wage a defensive war against the police, I think this is a very likely possibility. I know that people are psychologically and materially prepared to do this because it's becoming a matter of life and death. For instance, Bobby Hutton was murdered in Oakland on April 6. Here in a big area there have been about four other shootings and killings of young black men by police and so the last straw has already been placed on the camel's back. Unless these police departments are brought down to a level where they are acceptable

5

to a community, there can be nothing but a reply to them, in time; and it seems that that's the way it's going to be.

QUESTION: Tell me a little about the Peace and Freedom Party with which the Black Panther Party is working.

CLEAVER: The Peace and Freedom Party is composed primarily of white people who were disgusted by the two party system -- the so-called Republican and Democratic parties. They've broken away from those two parties, and the type of corrupt policies that they've been practicing since they've come into existence, and formed a new third party that seeks to align itself with the legitimate aspirations of the black community and with the anti-war movement in this country. It seems to chart a new direction in national politics. We felt that this was a positive sign coming out of the white community and we saw no reason not to work with them, because we share some of the same goals and attitudes.

QUESTION: Who do you think black people should support for president?

CLEAVER: I think you should support me for president. I am running against Dick Gregory on the Peace and Freedom Party ticket. Gregory, Dr. Benjamin Spock and Mrs. Coretta King has been proposed as possible nominees. I think I have it sewed up.

QUESTION: Do you think you'll get rid of Reagan in California?

CLEAVER: If we can't get rid of Reagan, we can't survive. Our survival depends upon getting rid of racist politicians like him.

QUESTION: Why did Dick Gregory call off the boycott of the Democratic National Convention in Chicago?

CLEAVER: Richard Gregory issued a public statement regarding that decision. He didn't want to be involved in any provocative situation that might lead to violence because a few things had happened about that time, I don't know if it was an uprising, or a shooting, or some event with overtones of violence. This was during the time when the racist pig, Mayor Richard Daley of Chicago, issued the orders to shoot and kill the black people if they were thought to be looting. Dick Gregory said he would cooperate in that effort; he didn't want to have anything to do with any trouble or uprising. This is a good example of the wishy-washy way Dick has always moved in those matters. This is one of the reasons I oppose his nomination for the Peace and Freedom Party. I wouldn't want to see his politics institutionalized.

QUESTION: Do you have any particular message for the Black college students as to what they could do to help benefit the whole of Black America?

I say to black students and potential students that they should return with their hearts and their minds and their souls to the black community to relate to the brothers and sisters who have not had the opportunity that they've had. They should use their intelligence and their skills to help organize the black community for it[s] survival. We are faced now with the prospects of oppression on an international level by a very racist and inhuman power structure which, as it winds up the war in Vietnam, turns to a second war, which is the war against black people right here in Babylon. I say to college students and to all people who want to see a new world and a better world that they should unite to form the type of power block that can defeat this racist power structure and put it in the garbage can of history where it belongs.

QUESTION: Don't you believe that Ghandi did a great deal more with non-violence?

CLEAVER: It may be. To a great extent he liberated his country with the use of non-violence, but he was dealing with people other than the racist yankees that we must confront here. He was dealing with a minority of occupying forces. We're dealing with the majority of a very complacent people who surround us, who have us dispersed throughout their population, who have a tradition of murdering and treating us in a very brutal and violence fashion, and who don't seem to be able to recognize the fact that black people have suffered beyond any more tolerance of a continuation of these conditions. To those who urge us to use adoptions from other lands, adoptions that in effect leave us merciless before very vicious enemies, we would say to them to take their non-violence and go preach it to the racist President of this country. Teach non-violence to LBJ. Teach non-violence to Chief Charles Gain, the number one pig in the Oakland Police Department. Teach nonviolence to the racist policemen all over this country who are murdering the children of black people. Don't come to the black community and teach the victims of this violence to be nonviolen[t]; teach the perpetrators of violence to be non-violent and then we can talk about it.

QUESTION: What would you recommend that the typical whites do to help you?

CLEAVER: I think any white person who is interested in the welfare of mankind should take a good look at what's going on in this country. This is what's really happening. The white students of this country have already taken a look at what's going on and they don't like it. So I say that they should organize themselves into machinery that will be capable of dealing with the revolution from what we call the white mother country. We feel that we have black people here who are colonized by the white people. We refer to that as the relationship between the black colony and the white mother country. We feel that we need to wage a national liberation struggle in the black colony and a revolution in the white mother country. Young white people are interested in doing this should organize themselves in a fashion to deal with the politics and the economics and the social practices in this country and should be prepared to work with those elements in the black community who understand this process, and who are willing to work with them. We think that with this type of coalition, we will have the strength to bring about the revolutionary changes that this country must have if there's going to be a future for our America or for mankind.

QUESTION: You talk about revolutionary changes. Let's see if your argument makes any sense. First of all, you've got to consider, if you talk about violence, what percentage of population is Negro in the United States, and you've got to recognize that you are outnumbered by about 10 to 1. You've also got to consider how many resources in the United States are Negro-controlled. How many factories, how many food-production arteries do you control? Do you own the trucking companies to get your men and machines from place-to-place, when the revolution takes place? How many airlines and how many communication systems are black controlled? You're asking black people to organize and be willing to die for the country.

CLEAVER: I also said kill, didn't I?

QUESTION: Kill and die. Well, that's a tremendous responsibility - you're asking them to kill and die.

CLEAVER: Let me ask you a question. Are you a white man or a black man?

QUESTION: I'm a white man, sir.

CLEAVER: I thought so. Let me tell you this. You can count off your statistics about everything that you control. And if you had it sewed up tight, then you shouldn't be concerned about what black people can do in this country. But we know that with all of your numbers and with all of your materials and superiorities, with all these things that you have going for you, you're in big trouble all over the planet earth. You dig it? We know that, and we don't look upon this situation as being just something confined to the geographical boundaries of the United States or the North American continent. We see this as a world-wide contest, and in this world-wide contest, you are in a very much of a minority, and we are with the majority. So you don't have 20 million black people to deal with, you have 700 million Chinese, 300 million Africans, and un-numbered billions, and millions and millions, and millions, and millions of mad black, brown, red, and yellow people to deal with. And you know that. We don't care about your atomic bombs. We don't care about your tanks, your guns and how many guns you have. Because when the push comes to shove, we would do the same thing that the Viet Cong is doing in Vietnam. We will lay and wait, and we will take your guns from you, and we will use your guns against you. Your plants and your factories are right here in our neighborhood. You put them there because you didn't want them in your own neighborhood, because they give out their smoke and those fowl[ul] smells. These resources are here and we will move against them and disrupt the economy of this country and force you to destroy all of your liberties and all the beautiful things that you love. In order to suppress the 20 million black people in this country, you are going to have to destroy this country, and we say that if we can't have freedom here, then let us be destroyed because you don't deserve it. If we can't be free, you don't deserve to even talk of freedom, and your numbers and all that. You're moving in a fog, and there ain't nobody digging it but you.

QUESTION: I'd just like to make one more point. You ask these people to kill and die because the white people in the United States are trying to suppress the black people. I don't think that's true. They may be trying to suppress you, but they're not trying to suppress black people. That's another thing. What percentage of the Negro population of these millions of people that you are talking about are sympathetic to your cause?

CLEAVER: I think they're all sympathetic.

QUESTION: It seems to me that before you can have people take other lives and be willing to give up theirs, you're going to have to at least come up with a logical, viable cause for them to die and kill.

CLEAVER: I think that we already have that cause.

QUESTION: How much of the so-called racial disorders is actually racial and how much of it, in your estimation, is economic? The philosophy of white supremacy (the whole concept of all non-white people being inferior to and servants of white people) is something that developed after whites came

11

out of Europe and began to travel around the world and to find all these people who didn't have the weapons that they had and who they were able to...

QUESTION: They have technological superiority...

CLEAVER: They had a type of unethical savagery. For instance, when the white man came to America and encountered the Indian, the red man tried to help him to survive. You know, they teach you that in school: The settlers were starving and the red men helped them. Well, it was just a difference in the type of background from which the people came: Backgrounds that enabled the whites to prey on their fellow man. It's very important that people understand that there is a distinction between the economics of the situation and the racism of the situation. Historically, we could say that economics were primary and that the racist philosophy that was developed later on was done to to justify the whole process of exploitation of the non-white people. As the Europeans began to colonize them in Asia and Africa, Latin America, and so forth, they developed this philosophy to justify what they were doing to these people, only after they started doing it. Now, everything about this country has been permeated by this philosophy in order to justify it. When people encounter this, they encounter a mixture of economic exploitation and racism. Economics and racism go handin-hand. People who confront this situation daily, and who haven't had time to elaborate studies of the situation, don't have time to distinguish between the economics and the racism.

QUESTION: Mr. Cleaver, if you're so unahppy with America, or if this nation is so unsatisfactory, why don't you go back to Africa?

CLEAVER: I think that after we send you back to Europe, we might go back to Africa.

QUESTION: The crime rate amongst the Negro is the highest as far as the United States is concerned, and I say that the black people are committing genocide against the white people.

CLEAVER: You can say that, if you want to. But I say that the crime rate, or what you call the crime rate, is not nearly high enough. Black people are put into a position where they either have to go out and beg you white people for things to survive, or they have to go out and take it. So I say they're not able to get it in any other way, that they should push the crime rate to high heavens and just take it all -- everything you've got. You don't deserve it, because you have an anti-human attitude toward other people.

QUESTION: I say, sir, that if anyone wants to work they can work.

CLEAVER: Do you know there are millions and millions of people in this country who want to work and who can't find jobs?

QUESTION: There are plenty of jobs available.

CLEAVER: Well, why don't you go out to one of the unemployment offices and tell those people who are standing in those lines that there are plenty of jobs available? Why don't you do that?

QUESTION: Well, the jobs are available, but they cannot guarantee help. And I think your violence polarizes the situation. You're not bringing the white people and black people together.

CLEAVER: We want to bring people together who have their heads together. It wouldn't be any good to bring people together who have their heads so untogether, you know.

13

QUESTION: Mr. Cleaver, does the Black Panther Party accept or welcome the help of white people?

CLEAVER: Yes, we work with white people all the time. We have good relations with a lot of white people. We have a coalition with the Peace and Freedom Party which, as I said earlier, is composed of white people. We work with different groups on the campuses, and with white people who have had a chance to see us in action and who know what we'v[r] e involved in and what our aims are. This is distinguished from the racists in the power structure who want to keep people divided. They don't want to see white people and black people work together on anything that seriously contests the status quo. They're the ones who spread racism through their control of the mass media; they try to spread the idea that the Black Panther Party is some type of irresponsible gang of hoodlums, whose only ambition is to go out and kill and murder and invade the suburbs and all that magic. But the white people here in this area work with us, and we do a very good job, and there's no problem in that area. Our problem comes from the racists who fear the development on a national scale of a working coalition between black people and white people who want to move to change this country. This is what they fear and this is why they move to suppress all tendencies and all manifestations of political expression that are moving in that direction. Any white person with any sense who wants to do something to bring about a better world, has never had a hard time talking to black people or relating to black people because black people have been so down on hatred, they have been so much the victims of racism and racial hatred that it's almost impossible for a

14

black person to really become a[s?] racist as white people are. This is not one of our problems.

QUESTION: Is it possible then that the white and black can live together?

CLEAVER: If you're speaking in ultimate terms as to whether it will be ultimately possible for white people and black people to live together, I think it will be up to white people. Black people are willing to live side-by-side with other people. But the question is this, how are we to move and survive against a hostile population that on the one hand sends in a few of its numbers to talk non-violence to us, to talk brotherhood to us, and to talk about living together, while on the other hand the very working and functioning of this system is daily grinding black people down and keeping them down? While other people's standard of living is going up, ours is falling or standing still. It's very difficult for us to be concerned about brotherhood when we see the operation of this country destroying us.

QUESTION: What do you mean when you talk about black? Is this a descendent from Africa, or is it a Negro, or is it everyone that is non-white?

CLEAVER: You know the saying: if you have one drop of black blood in you, you're not white. You know how white people run around saying that. Well, they were classifying the various people as not belonging to their superior group. But we have people in our group who run from those who can pass for white, you know, like Adam Clayton Powell, who could very well be a white man, or from Senator Brooks on down to brothers and sisters who are pure black and who have never had their blood lines corrupted. We all are descendents of the people who were brought here from the mother-land and fatherland of Africa.

QUESTION: Would you include some like a Mexican-American or an Indian as black? You say black is a descendent from Africa.

CLEAVER: Yes, we do include that as a descendent of Africa because Africa is the home of the black man. The Mexican people refer to themselves as brown people, and I've heard Indian people refer to themselves as the red man.

QUESTION: You use the simile, then, about your brothers in China. Yet, they're not black.

CLEAVER: I didn't say my black brothers in China; I said my brothers in China. They're my yellow brothers if you want me to be specific.

QUESTION: If the Black Panther Party was to decide to forego the idea of defensive measures, do you think there would be more acceptance of the party?

CLEAVER: Yes, I think that a lot of people would see that as a good sign, but I think there actually would be a very great disservice to mankind, for if we abandoned our position of calling for a cessation of the brutality and terror of black people, then we would, in effect, be endorsing evil. And we say that it is the duty of people to stand up and to impeccably oppose all manifestations of inhuman behavior. Transcriber's comment (February 5, 2005): Today, the majority of Black people do not support a revolutionary party like the BPP even though it could be in their interests. However, what Cleaver says below about the oppressed minority of Amerikans being part of the world majority, who are oppressed by imperialism, is correct. Imperialism is doomed despite its "numbers ... ma-

16

terials and superiorities" in the imperialist country. The below article show's the BPP's internationalism and anti-Menshevism. Cleaver mentions Ghandi. It has to be pointed out Mao's approach would have been better than Ghandi's even in India precisely because the enemy was a minority of the population. It's not that MIM is pacifist, or pseudo-pacifist like Ghandi, but "in the current strategic stage of struggle MIM advocates only protracted legal struggle in the imperialist countries and internal semi-colonies. The exception to this is of First Nations bordering imperialist countries which can form their own police and army."

2. Imperialism, Economics and Heart Transplants by Landon Williams. October 5, 1968

Plainly put, imperialism is a system whos[se] main concern is the profit. Without something or someone to exploit, imperialism would soon die and perish into dust. These are true facts independent of man's arguments. The first regard of imperialist [s] is always with getting the most profits and most usefulness out of everything. Oil is one example of what that means and the use of the hog is another. Oil is used for many purposes other than putting in cars for joyriding. Plastics, some synthetic fabrics, bug spray and even imitation flavorings for ice cream are made from oils. On the hog everything is used in some way, the guts, the brain, the tongue, and even the vital organs. Imperialism makes the most economic use of all its materials and wastes nothing. Some of the things Black revolutionaries have used to try and wake up some of our dreaming brothers and breakdown the myth of Black people ever being assimilated into America's imperialist system, has been the fact that Black people everyday are becoming less of an asset and more and more of a deficit here in racist America and the fact that racist U.S. imperialism in Viet Nam, when faced with losing its profits, has falsely thought it more economical to try to destroy people of color than to risk profits with them around. Some of our brothers and sisters however refuse to believe these facts and [refuse to] recognize the real danger that this situation presents to Black people. Some even go so far as to spout forth such insane things as "America can't do without the Black man, she needs us." By this, I take it that they mean it would be uneconomical for America to get rid of the Black man because to think of America needing us in anyway other than dollars and cents or profit motives would be unrealistic and completely opposite to the true nature of American imperialism. After observing the latest medical developments and most recently what took place last week I hate to admit it but they may be right. It may be a decadent America's interests to keep the Black man around. A white "doctor" from racist Nazi-like South Africa seems to have found a very economical and profitable answer to the problem of what to do with Black people. Last week Sept 8-14, Dr. Christian Bernard succeeded once again in making medical history and doing another barbaric act reminiscent of Hitler's mad doctors. His feat was shockingly ghastly and showed the true savage nature of racist imperialism. Dr. Christian Bernard ripped the life giving heart from the breast of a pregnant Black woman and transplanted it into the cancer infested chest of a racist white pig. The details weren't fully released though the regular newspapers and only one radio station carried a partial report of the story. Dr. Bernard was being very economical; indeed he succeeded in killing three birds with one stone. That is he one: aided in the genocide racist imperialism is waging against people of color by murdering a fertile young Black woman, two, he eliminated the future threat that the yet to be born black child might have presented to racist imperialism by dealing with the child in typical cowardly racist manner and snuffing the life out of the unborn Black child in its mother's womb, and thirdly, he extended the life of a decaying white pig in Nazi South Africa. Black people everywhere in the world and especially here in cancerous decaying America, must begin to pay closer attention to what's being done, all around us, in white christian countries, in the name of "medical science" and "humanity". Black people must begin to analyze what's happening everywhere around us. When we realize that the only logic imperialism follows is the logic of profit and loss, then perhaps the reasons why so many white "christian" Americans, after 100 years, are suddenly so against black seperation will become much clearer. Perhaps it is not that they believe so much in intergration, as they insist, or equality but rather that they, like Dr. Christian Bernard see the usefulness of keeping Black people handy as a ready supply of spare parts. Anyway with the rate that heart disease and lung cancer deaths are increasing and with the enormous profits to be made from cancer ridden pigs, who wish to extend their lives, it would beho [o] ve each of us, when we feel ourselves being watched by the pigs, if we think not only of the immediate and obvious threat to our lives that they constitute armed with their guns and tanks, but also think of the su[b]tler but far more gruesome threat of Tule Lake, the Stanford Medical Center and Heart-transplants.

21

3. TIRANA DENOUNCES SOVIET-U.S. INTRIGUE.
OCTOBER 12, 1968. PAGE 8.

TIRANA - Today's "bashkimi" (unity) in a commentary entitled "Thirty Years After Munich" strongly denounced Soviet revisionism and U.S. Imperialism for their collusion to re-divide the world into their spheres of influence and to plot another Munich. The commentary says that thirty years after the notorious Munich treaty, the Czechoslovak people are today again trampled under the iron heels of foreign aggressors, their national interests once again becoming the commodity in the transactions among big powers.

4. Anti-U.S. Rallies. October 19, 1968. Page 4

Peking, October 8 - Japanese workers, peasants and students held anti-U.S. rallies and demonstrations simultaneously in Tokyo, Osaka, Saitama, and Fukuoka on October 6, demanding the dismantling of the Japan-U.S. "Security Treaty," according to a Toho news agency report.

The rally in Tokyo of about 1,000 workers and students was held at a place designated for the expansion of the Tachikawa U.S. Air Base. After the rally, the participants held an impressive demonstration at the shopping center near the base. Despite the annoying roaring of low-flying U.S. planes, the workers, peasants and students persisted in holding the rally. Speakers at the rally wrathfully condemned the U.S. imperialist war of aggression against Viet Nam and voiced their determination to struggle to the end against U.S. bases. A worker read out the inscription written by Chairman Mao for Japanese worker friends: "The Japanese revolution will undoubtedly be victorious, provided the universal truth of Marxism-Leninism is really integrated with the concrete practice of the Japane se revolution." He said: "We must study this inscription seriously." Let us firmly arm ourselves with Mao Tse-tung's thought and strive to win final victory. After the rally, the workers and students staged a militant demonstration around the base. Marching at the head were demonstrators holding red banners inscribed with the slogan: "Long Live Mao Tse-Tung's Thought!" They appealed to the citizens to fight together with them for the dismantling of U.S. military bases. In Saitama Prefecture, about 300 young workers and students held a rally in Osaka City where a U.S. army field hospital and the offices of the U.S. information service are located. The demonstrations expressed the determination to carry on till victory, the struggle for the abrogation of the Japan-U.S. "Security Treaty" and for the dismantling of U.S. military bases. After the rally, the participants held a demonstration and fought fiercely with 500 police sent by the reactionary Sato government. In Ibaraki Prefecture, about 5,000 workers, students and other citizens held a rally and demonstration in Katsuta City demanding the immediate dismantling of the U.S. military base in the city and opposing the building of a nuclear fuel reprocessing plant in Tokai Village outside the city. About 400 young workers, students and other citizens held a rally near the U.S. army field hospital in Yokihama City to demand the removal of the hospital. The rally was followed by a demonstration. About 200 young workers and students from Kansai Area held a rally and demonstration in Toyonaka City, Osaka Prefecture, expressing their determination to struggle for the restoration of diplomatic relations between Japan and China and the smashing of the Japan-U.S. "Security Treaty."

Some 300 workers held a rally in front of Yamada ammunition depot of the U.S. air base in Kitakyushu City, Fukuoka Prefecture, to demand the immediate dismantling of the depot. A vigorous demonstration was held after the rally.

5. MEXICAN STUDENT STRUGGLE SHAKES LATIN AMERICA

MEXICO CITY – The Mexican students have been heroically waging an unprecedentedly fierce struggle against the reactionary authorities' barbarous suppression and cruel persecution and bloody slaughter. This storm of large-scale mass struggle is powerfully battering the rule of the Mexican monopoly capitalist class and is shaking the whole continent of Latin America–the "back yard" of U.S. imperialism. This struggle began with the general strike and big demonstrations launched by the students in Mexico City, the capital of Mexico, in late July in protest against the suppression of the student movement and the barbarous persecution of progressive students by the so-called "riot squad". These police-attacks on students came during demonstrations celebrating the July 26th anniversary of the Cuban Revolution. As the reactionary troops and police stepped up their sanguinary suppression of the student movement, the student struggle against persecution and slaughter developed swiftly and became stronger and stronger. Our great teacher Chairman Mao says: "The young people are the most active and vital force in society." The struggle waged by the revolutionary Mexican youth fully proves the correctness of Chairman Mao's wise thesis. The student struggle was focused on protesting against the criminal suppression of the student movement and persecution of progressive students perpetrated by the so-called "riot squad," which were directly trained by the U.S. imperialists for the sole purpose of suppressing the progressive mass movement. At the very beginning of the struggle, the students raised sharp political demands such as: "Disband the riot squad", "Abrogate the Laws which suppress the people's movement," "set free the political prisoners, release the arrested students, punish the murderers, and give relief funds to the families of the victims". The just struggle is being waged by patriots of various social strata. The struggle developed rapidly and vigorously and surged forward wave upon wave. It started from Mexico City, and spread to Nuevo Leon and more than ten other states and several important cities. It began with the student strikes and developed into large-scale demonstrations and mass rallies held by hundreds of thousands of workers, peasants, teachers and patriots from various circles. 200,000 students, workers and peasants in the capital held an impressive demonstration on August 27 to protest against the brutal police suppression. As the demonstrators marched through the streets, many passers-by repeatedly shouted their support to the demonstrators. This was the largest mass demonstration in Mexico in the past decades. After the outbreak of the struggle, the Mexican students waged a tit-for-tat struggle against the brutalities of the reactionary troops and police. They occupied the campuses of universities and colleges, threw up barricades in the streets, and hit back at the reactionary troops and police with stones, clubs and incendiary bottles. The most bitter struggle took place in Mexico City. For more than two months, university and middle school students hold a series of strikes, protesting against the Mexican authorities for ruthlessly repressing the progressive students. In defiance of brute force, the students fought valiantly and fiercely against the fully armed troops and police, who on some occasions called out armored cars and helicopters and even used bazookas against the students. On July 26, when tens of thousands of students in the Mexican capital held a demonstration and parade in honor of the Cuban Revolution, the authorities called out a large number of troops and police to disperse the demonstrating students. But the students fought back bravely; they overturned cars and threw up barricades, waging a pitched battle against the reactionary troops and police. When thousands of Mexico City students held another demonstration on the night of July 29 and marched towards the U.S. Embassy, the reactionary troops and police committed a more savage repression. Early the next morning, they opened fire with bazookas to blast open the gate of a middle school where demonstrating students were assembled, then charged in with clubs and barbarously attacked the students. The intensified repression aroused stiffer resistance from the students. Beginning August 5, the students of the Capital held a series of demonstrations in which tens of thousands took part. On August 13, some 80,000 students in Mexico City, scorning the intimidation of the reactionary authorities, held a parade, the columns of which extended for more than five kilometres, and staged a grand rally at the "Central Square" (Zocalo) near the National Palace, to strongly protest against the brutalities committed by the troops and police against the students. The demonstration thus pushed to a new high the struggle against persecution and repression.

6. In Defense Of Self Defense.
Exclusive By Huey Newton. November 16, 1968.
Page 12

(Huey on Anarchists and Individualists as related to revolutionary struggle and the Black Liberation Movement) We should understand there is a difference between the rebellion of the anarchists and the black revolution or liberation of the black colony. This is a class society; it always has been. This reactionary class society places its limitation on individuals, not just in terms of their occupation, but also regarding self expression, being mobile, and being free to really be creative and do anything they want to do. The class society prevents this. This is true not only for the mass of the lower or subjugated class. It is also true within the ruling class, the master class. That class also limits the freedom of the individual souls of the people which comprise it. In America, we have not only a class society, we also have a caste system and black people are fitted into the lowest caste. They have no mobility for going up the class ladder. They have no privilege to enter the ruling structure at all. Within the ruling class they're objecting (resisting?), because the people have found that they're completely subjected to the will of the administration and to the

31

manipulators. This brings about a very strange phenomenon in America, that is, many of th e rebelling white students and the anarchists are the offspring of this master class. Surely most of them have a middle class background and some even upper class. They see the limitations imposed upon them and now they're striving, as all men strive, to get freedom of the soul, freedom of expression, and freedom of movement without the artificial limitations from antique values. Blacks and colored people in America, confined within the caste system, are discriminated against as a whole group of people. It's not a question of individual freedom as it is for the children of the upper classes. We haven't reached the point of trying to free ourselves individually because we're dominated and oppressed as a group of people. Part of the people of this country - which is a great part- are part of the youth themselves. But they're not doing this as a group of people because, as a group, they're already free to an extent. Their problem is not a group problem really, because they can easily integrate into the structure. Potentially, they're mobile enough to do this: they're the educated ones, the "future of the country," and so forth. They can really gain a certain amount of power over the society by integrating into the rulership circle.

But they see that even within the rulership circle, there are still antique values that have no respect for individualism. They find themselves subjugated. No matter what class they're in, they find themselves subjugated because of the nature of this class society. So their fight is to free the individual's soul. This brings about another problem. They're being ruled by an alien source that has nothing to do with freedom of individual expression. They want to escape this, to overturn this, but they see no need to form a structure or a real, disciplined vanguard movement. Their reasoning is that, by setting up a disciplined organization, they feel they'd be replacing the old structure with other limitations. They fear they'd be setting themselves up as directing the people, therefore limiting the individual again. But what they don't understand, or it seems that they don't understand, is that as long as the military-industrial complex exists, the structure of oppression of the individual will continue. An individual would be threatened even if he were to achieve t he freedom he's seeking. He'll be threatened because there will be an organized lower group there ready to strip him of his individual freedom at any moment. In Cuba they had a revolution, they had a vanguard group that was a disciplined group, and they realized that the state won't disappear until imperialism is completely wiped out, structurally and also philosophically, or the bourgeois thoughts won't be changed. Once imperialism is wiped out they can have their communist state and the state or territorial boundaries will disappear. In this country the anarchists seem to feel that if they just express themselves individually and tend to ignore the limitations imposed on them, without leadership and without discipline, they can oppose the very disciplined, organized, reactionary state . This is not true. They will be oppressed as long as imperialism exists. You cannot oppose a system such as this without opposing it with organization that's even more extremely disciplined and dedicated than the structure you're opposing. I can understand the anarchists wanting to go directly from state to non-state, but historically it's incorrect. As far as I'm concerned, thinking of the recent French Revolution, the reason the French uprising failed is simply because the anarchists in the country, who by definition had no organization, had no people that were reliable enough, as far as the mass of the people were concerned, to replace DeGaulle and his government. Now, the people were skeptical about the Communist Party and the other progressive parties because they didn't side with the people of medium living. They lagged behind the people, so they lost the respect of the people and the people looked for guidance from the students and anarchists.

But the anarchists were unable to offer a structural program to replace the DeGaulle government. So the people were forced to turn back to DeGaulle. It wasn't the people's fault; it was CohnBendit's fault and all the other anarchists who felt they could just go from state to non-state. In this country - getting back home to North America now - we can side with the student radicals. We would try to encourage them and persuade them to organize and weld a sharp cutting tool. In order to do this they would have to be disciplined and they would have at least some philosophical replacement of the system. This is not to say that this itself will free the individual. The individual will not be free until the state does not exist at all, and I think - I don't want to be redundant - this cannot be replaced by the anarchists right away. As far as the blacks are concerned, we are not hung up on attempting to actualize or express our individual souls because we're oppressed not as individuals but as a whole group of people. Our evolution, or our liberation, is based first on freeing our group, freeing our group to a certain degree. After we gain our liberation, our people will not be free. I can imagine in the future that the blacks will rebel against the organized leadership that the blacks themselves have structured. They will see there will be limitations, limiting their individual selves, and limiting their freedom of expression. But this is only after they become free as a group. This is what makes our group different from the white anarchists - besides he views his group as already free. Now he's striving for freedom of his individual self. This is the big difference. We're not fighting for freedom of our individual selves, we 're fighting for a group freedom. In the future there will probably be a rebellion where blacks will say, "Well, our leadership is limiting our freedom because of the rigid discipline. Now that we've gained our freedom, we will strive for our individualistic freedom that has nothing to do with organized group or state." And the group will be disorganized, and it should be. But at this point we stress discipline, we stress organization, we do not stress psychodelic drugs and all the other things that have to do with just the individual expansion of the mind. We're trying to gain true liberation of a group of people, and this makes our struggle somewhat different from the whites. Now, how is it the same? It's the same in the fact that both of us are striving for freedom. They will not be free - the white anarchists will not be free - until we are free so that makes our fight their fight, really. The imperialists and the bourgeois bureaucratic capitalistic system would not give them individual freedom while they keep a whole group of people based upon race or color oppressed as a group. How can they expect to get individual freedom when the imperialists oppress whole nations of people? Until we gain liberation as a group, they won't gain any liberation as individual people. So this makes our fight the same, and we must keep this in perspective and always see the similarities and the differences in it. There's a tremendous amount of difference in it, and there's a due amount of similarity between the two cases. Both are striving for freedom and both are striving for liberation of their people, only one is advanced to a degree higher than the other. The anarchists are advanced a step higher, but only in theory. As far as actuality of conditions, they shouldn't be advanced higher because they should see the necessity of wiping out the imperialistic structure by organized groups just as we must be organized.

7. New Zealand Hails Triumph Of China's Cultural Revolution
December 21, 1968. Page 18

Wellington -- The political committee of the Communist Party of New Zealand, in a statement in the "People's Voice" today, warmly acclaims the great proletarian cultural revolution in China and the great victory of the enlarged Twelfth Plenary Session of the Eighth Central Committee of the Communist Party of China. The statement says, "An intense struggle is being waged between two powerful forces in the international arena. One of these forces represents the toiling and oppressed people of the world. The other represents the exploiters and oppressors." It continues, "At the head of the alliance of all the exploited classes and nations stands revolutionary China, under the leadership of the Lenin of our time, Chairman Mao Tse-tung. At the head of the other alliance of exploiters and traitors to socialism stand the imperialist leaders and Soviet revisionist leaders. "The struggle between the two totally opposed forces is going on in all countries of the world, including New Zealand. Every victory for the forces of revolutionary socialism and national liberation is a victory for the working class and exploited of New Zealand against the people's enemies. "For this reason, the political committee applauds the triumph of the proletarian cultural revolution in China, which has kept China firmly on the path of evolutionary socialism against all attempts from within and without to turn China back to capitalism ." the statement emphasizes.

It points out that the schemes of China's arch revisionist Liu Shao-chi to restore capitalism have been thoroughly smashed by the revolutionary workers and peasants of China under the wise leadership of Chairman Mao Tse-tung and the people of China. This is a victory of the working people of all countries.

8. MAURITANIAN PEOPLE. DECEMBER 21, 1968. PAGE 18

NOUAKCHOTT - Mauritanian army men and civilians held a parade here today warmly celebrating the eighth anniversary of the independence of the Islamic Republic of Mauritania. Mauritanian President Moktar Ould Daddah reviewed the parade. The paraders held placards bearing slogans: "Americans get out of Viet Nam which belongs to the Vietnamese people," "People's war is the only road for the liberation of Arab Palestine," and "Fully support the fraternal Arab peoples in opposing imperialism and zionism." At a session of the National Assembly after the parade, President Daddah delivered a speech in which he reviewed the achievements of the Mauritanian people in the past year in developing the national economy and in consolidating their national independence, as well as in other spheres. Referring to Mauritania's foreign policy, he declared: "So long as we are united, we can struggle more effectively against colonialism and neo-colonialism which are enslaving our African brothers." Praising the relations of friendship and cooperation between Mauritania and China, President Daddah said, "Our cooperation with the People's Republic of China has entered a positive and fruitful stage." The President condemned U.S. imperialism for waging a war of aggression against Viet Nam and denounced Israeli zionism, a product of imperialism, for forcibly occupying Arab land. He declared that the Mauritanian people support the just struggle of the Palestinian and other Arab people against imperialism and colonialism.

9. REPARATIONS FOR VIETNAM.
JANUARY 4, 1969. PAGE 7.

At least a million Vietnamese people have been killed by the Americans or by puppet forces armed and directed by the U.S. Precious human lives can never be replaced with money or goods. Yet material compensation must be granted to the survivors. Using the racist standards of imperialism, the U.S. government has paid $34 per person to relatives of persons killed by its armed forced "by accident" in so-called "friendly areas." Such token payments measure nothing but the depravity of the U.S. military rules. Here is a suggested standard. The U.S. grants each serviceman a $10,000 life insurance policy, for a token premium of $2 yearly. This maybe taken as the minimum value of a human life. Applied to the million plus killed by U.S. imperialism in Vietnam, it comes to a total of more than $10 billion.

10. Indian Magazine Denounces Revisionism January 4, 1969. Page 8.

New Delhi (Pan. African Press) - The Indian Monthly *Liberation* published an article in its latest issue condemning the Soviet revisionist renegade clique for betraying the road of the October Revolution. It also denounced the Dange renegade clique in India and the revisionists of India for their counter-revolutionary crimes. The article said: "By using the State machine, the Soviet revisionist renegade clique, headed by Krushchev and his successors, Kosygin and Brezhnev, has restored capitalism in the Soviet Union and itself practices neo-capitalism." The article stated that the Soviet revisionist renegade clique's "invasion of Czechoslovakia conclusively proves that this clique has degenerated into social-fascism and social-imperialism." It said: "This revisionist renegade clique is the sworn enemy not only of the Soviet working people, but of all the workers and oppressed nations of the world including the Indian people." The article denounced the Dange renegade clique and the revisionists of India for stubbornly opposing the path of the Naxalbari armed revolution. It said that after the Twentieth Congress of the C.P.S.U., they have openly renounced the path of the October Revolution, the path of violent revolution, and have been trying their utmost to lead the Indian revolutionary people astray by advocating the peaceful "parliamentary road." It said that the Dange renegade and the revisionists of India have openly stood on the side of the domestic reactionaries, the Soviet revisionist renegade clique and the U. S. imperialists. They have degenerated into the running dogs of the U. S. imperia lism and Soviet revisionism and lackeys of the big Indian landlords and bourgeoisie. The rising tide of the Indian revolution will sweep them away like garbage, however, widely they may now rage against the peasant struggle and against socialist China.

11. WATER SHORTAGE IN INDIA.
JANUARY 4, 1969. PAGE 8

NEW DELHI -- A large part of India's Rajasthan State is hit by a devastating drought and the reactionary Indian ruling circles' cruel exploitation and apathy have added much suffering to the people there. Indian newspapers reported recently that heavy drought hit the entire Western and Northwestern Rajasthan, especially five districts bordering on Pakistan. Nearly 3 million people, or one third of the state's population, were seriously affected. Poor peasants were forced to leave their villages, and in October, about one million villagers were roaming the cities and towns in search of work. Many of them especially children were starved to death. A large number of cattle died of shortage of wate r and fodder. In some villages carcasses of oxen piled up like hills. Rain is the main source of water supply. But all tanks and reservoirs for collecting rain water had dried up. Under the ruthless exploitation by the reactionary Indian authorities, the people could not afford to dig enough wells. In the Jaisalmer district, 200,000 people needed about 100 tube-wells. They only received 10 working ones. They had to share their ration, with their cattle, which they received on alternate days. Food rations for the people in the drought-stricken areas fell far short of demand. The local princely families, though, had huge stocks of food-grains and fodder. So did the big landlords and usurers. With the help of the local bureaucrats they sold food-grains at high prices to make fabulous profits from the misery of the people. The reactionary Indian government forced the people, thousands of hungry people, including women and small children to build military roads. They were treated cruelly by foremen; wages were withheld for weeks. Diseases were high as a result of the starvation and hot weather. The reactionary Indian authorities provided no medical facilities for the people. They even refused it. In Sangarh, a place in the drought-affected areas, a village woman was desperately looking for a doctor to cure her sick, four month old child. A government doctor refused to let her bring the child near him.

12. JAPANESE STUDENTS.
JANUARY 4, 1969. PAGE 8.

TOKYO (Third-World Press) - The patriotic Japanese students of Ryukyu University held a rally and demonstration in Naha City, Okinawa prefecture last week to voice their strong demand for the withdrawal of the bandit B-52 bombers of the U.S. armed pig forces now stationing in Okinawa. Following the explosion of a B-52 shortly after taking off from the Kadena base in Okinawa last month which resulted in injuring a number of local residents and damaging their houses, another incident took place in the same base last week when one of the B-52 bombers made an emergency landing after it took off. Furious over the incident, about three hundred students of Ryukyu University held a rally in front of the U.S. Civil Administration in Naha City to express their determination to struggle resolutely for the withdrawal of B-52 bombers from Okinawa and the dismantling of U.S. military bases in the island. Right after the rally, the students staged a demonstration, marching in high spirits to the Kadena U.S. military base. They shouted such anti-U.S. slogans as "Withdraw immediately the B-52 bombers," and "Smash the Japan-U.S. 'Security Treaty'." Merging with another group of people demonstrating in front of the base, they condemned the crimes committed by the U.S. bandit planes. The forceful action of the students threw the U.S. and Japanese reactionary pigs into a panic. The latter sent out about five hundred armed policemen to ruthlessly suppress the demonstrators. Braving the pigs' brutal suppression, the students stormed the base several times and fought bravely with the police.

13. NAGA ARMED FORCES. JANUARY 4, 1969. PAGE 8.

NEW DELHI - The armed forces of the Naga people, in defiance of the armed suppression by the reactionary Indian government, have in the past few months seized favorable opportunities in mounting repeated attacks on the enemy and fought them heroically. On December 12, the Naga armed forces in Tengnoupal area of the Union Territory Manipur launched a surprise attack on the unit of reactionary Indian police, killing four armed police and wounding six. All the arms and ammunition of the police unit were captured. In early September of this year, the Naga armed forces laid an ambush and killed three officers of the Indian troops, including a captain. In the middle of October, the Naga armed forces using automatic weapons opened heavy fire on a patrol unit of the Indian security force near Tungam, Manipur. On October 23, the Naga armed forces in the vicinity of this place again attacked the reactionary Indian police forces. Indian army chief-of-staff Kumaramanglam hurriedly rushed to Kohima, capital of Nagaland, on November 7 to make arrangements for suppressive measures. It was revealed that in mid-November the reactionary Indian government sent large numbers of troops to Nagaland from the military centers of Assam state. The reactionary Indian government also tried hard to sabotage the unity of the Naga people. It even provoked armed conflict among them in an attempt to quench the flames of their armed struggle. The Nagas harbor great enmity and hatred against the Indian reactionaries. For years the reactionary Indian troops and police have frantically massacred the Naga people, compelling them to go into the forests and take up arms for self-defense. Now the Nagas are strengthening their cooperation with the Mizos, Kukis and other nationalities, and are gradually uniting with the revolutionary peasants in East India who have risen to resist the reactionary Indian authorities and feudal landlords. The Nagas are expanding the scale of their armed struggle and dealing increasingly vigorous blows at the Indian reactionaries.

14. PEKING BUILDS LARGEST TANZANIA TEXTILE MILL
JANUARY 15, 1969. PAGE 3.

DAR ES SALAAM, AFRICA –(TNS)–"Bridgehead" and "Foothold" are two of the favorite words used (especially in American parlance) to describe the Chinese penetration into Tanzania. Each new arrival from Peking, whether a group of doctors for the bushland or surveyors for a promised railway link to Zambia is chronicled as further evidence of the "Yellow Peril." This type of catalogue usually omits the fact that there are more Canadians than Chinese in Tanzania, and if you totalled all the Western "experts," advisors, teachers, diplomats and missionaries, the Chinese are outnumbered by 20 to 1. Nevertheless to a Western world that is conditioned to see nothing but evil emanating from China, the Chinese presence here can be made to look pretty menacing. But a look at the large new textile mill completely built and financed by China, which was opened recently by President Nyerere, is a revelation of just how appropriate and how influential some forms of Chinese aid can be. As textile factories go, the Friendship Mill on the outskirts of Dar es Salaam is probably very ordinary and not too different from spinning, weaving and dyeing mills anywhere. Its real significance is that it is here. Tanzania has for

51

several years been a large producer of raw cotton, but it has always been shipped overseas for processing to be brought back as finished cloth and clothing at many times the cost. Now Tanzanians can see their own cotton being turned into their own clothing, especially the brightly colored shawls called "khangas", which are the basic female garments for most of the population. But any textile mill could do that. Although the Chinese mill is the largest and the first integrated complex that can also print designs on cotton as well as weave and dye it, it is not the first nor the only textile mill here. Why, then, is the Friendship Mill so different? Stories abound about Communist aid projects in the developing world that are badly designed and hurriedly built which have turned out to be useless. But this mill began production 18 months after the cornerstone was laid. Throughout this period, when China was apparently in chaos because of the cultural revolution, every shipment for the project arrived on schedule, right down to the fluorescent light bulbs. Nor is the machinery second-hand or jerry-built. It is all new, with metric markings in Chinese and English and there is a provision for quality control checks at every step. The Chinese knew enough about the climate to provide for air-conditioning and humidity controlled areas. Certainly the equipment is not as technologically sophisticated or automated as in the United States, but this is an advantage rather than a disadvantage. It provides more jobs in an area of high unemployment. Secondly the machinery is easier to understand and repair. Because any particular process is broken down into more steps than in an automated mill, it serves a valuable educational function, in a population where large numbers have never opened a door latch or threaded a nut.

Since the days of the "spinning jenny," textile has been the first form of industrialization and so it is a very appropriate beginning for a country like Tanzania. But it is not the technical functioning of a mill that is so impressive because it is probably a standard export model. Rather, it is the internal organization. The essential thing is that Tanzanians have been left to make the decisions themselves and consequently they are learning from their own mistakes. Compare this with the traditional system of investment in developing countries. All the executive personnel are foreigners while the local population provides cheap labor and raw materials. As long as there is a foreign financial interest[,] that [there? —Transcriber] will be a white manager, whereas the manager of the Friendship Mill is black from "day one." By the same token, the Friendship Mill is owned by Tanzania from the beginning, built with an interest[-]free loan whereas the traditional capitalist investor is allowed to send his profits out of the country, adding to the foreign exchange problems. Much has also been made of the Chinese shoulder-to-shoulder approach to training and that the Chinese work along with their Tanzanian counterparts rather than acting as supervisors. The personnel manager boasted that there is a Tanzanian understudying every Chinese workman at the mill. The Chinese actually getting their hands dirty demonstrates the basic difference between the Western and Eastern styles of giving foreign aid. When the Chinese come, they bring not only their engineers and technicians but also their own plumbers, carpenters, cooks, drivers and laborers. When a Western company undertakes a project it only sends supervisory personnel. What political and social impact will the presence of the Chinese make on

Tanzanians, or in Reader's Digest sentiments, will the Chinese win the battle for their hearts and minds? Just as I was leaving the mill a group of Chinese girls were lining up for lunch. Their square-cut hair, bra-less figures and baggy trousers were marked contrast to the Tanzanian girls, who love the bright colors they are helping to produce and who use newly found foundation garments and hair styles to best advantage. I doubt if they will be very anxious to emulate their Chinese sisters. President Nyerere himself has often said that his people are not prepared to accept the regimentation of the Chinese way of life.

But Chinese projects such as this will continue to be attractive to the African leaders, who see the Chinese actually demonstrating the devotion, hard work and frugality which everybody says is necessary but is very seldom found in practice.

15. Panther Purge. January 25, 1969. Page 17
By Virtual Murrell

The governing body of the Black Panther Party, which is our Central Committee, has decided that in order to preserve democratic centralism and to destroy ultra-democracy within our ranks, that it is of absolute necessity to understand the decadence of ultra-democracy. First, it must be crystal clear that ultra-democracy damages the party organization and seeks to undermine the Party. We must also point out that the petty bourgeoisie's individualistic aversion to discipline is directly related. They are not only practicing ultra-democracy, but they are opportunistic, and these individuals are not only opportunistic or counter-revolutionaries, but individuals who are renegades, jacknapes, and factionalizers who, with their obvious stupidity, try to divide our people by their very action. It is necessary for the Black Panther Party to expose those fools that go against the Party's rules. They exhibit without doubt that their personal opportunistic gain is worth more than the liberation of black people. It is necessary for the Black Panther Party, which is a People's Party, to purge members within the Party to rid ourselves of opportunism, the petty-bourgeoisie desires. You see, we believe in the teachings of our leader; the Minister of Defense, Huey P. Newton of the Black Panther Party, when he says, "Have faith in the party and have faith in the people." If the masses are going to have faith in the party, it's necessary and an absolute principle that we are very sincere and honest with the people, because it is necessary to restore the much needed trust and dedication which has been lacking for hundreds of years. If we, as the vanguard, failed to criticize and denounce buffoons, and simpletons, then we will be put into a position of hypocrisy. In actuality, we would be the fools for allowing it to exist without moving to remove those who aspire to opportunism, filthy reprobates.

Purging is a process which must be used, as "defined," as a cleansing process. In view of what has happened in the past, it was very clear that it was necessary to purge those who by their very overt actions try to destroy the Party and the Party's image. One of our objectives is to build and to unite black people and to lift their level of consciousness. In conclusion, we say that all those who aspire to opportunism are directly related to the repudiation of the dictatorship of the proletariat, which simply means "Power by the People." It is an unmistakable sign of treason in the highest form, betrayal of black people. All Power To the People. Black Power to Black People.

16. What Is Ultra-Democracy? February 2, 1969.
Page 14. By Field Marshal

D.C. Ultra-Democracy is individualism manifesting itself as an aversion to discipline. Our Minister of Defense, Huey P. Newton, pointed out in his essay on Anarchists and Individualists that, "This is a class society; it always has been." The majority of the people that become Panthers are from the lowest class. One of the major characteristics of this class is to think and act as an individual. This tendency was, and is, perpetrated by the ruling class (capitalists) in its rhetoric and in its governmental documents such as the declaration of independence, constitution, bill of rights, etc. Having people thinking and acting individually is an aid to the ruling class in its exploitation and oppression of people around the world in general, and the exploitation and oppression and the perpetration of racism against Black people in particular. All laws and institutions of the society are structured to create individual thinking and action. This prevents oppressed and exploited people from seeing their problem as a collective one, such as the exploitation and racism perpetuated against all Blacks. Therefore, collective thinking and action is required if oppressed and exploited people are to wage a successful struggle to gain their freedom and liberation. All things having a dual nature, let us examine what can be called the positive aspects of individualism on the part of the masses of Black people in this present society. Due to exploitation, oppression and racism of this society, the masses of Black people are mainly unemployed or under-employed. Therefore, means of survival other than employment were developed by Black people. Prime Minister Stokley Carmichael says, "You get things three ways: you work, you beg, or you take." Although Black people employ all three methods to fulfill their desires and needs, the latter receives priority. Many Black people become very revolutionary in the process in their action if not in their thought. They develop ways of surviving on this society but not in this society. This is done individually or in very small groups, never collectively. These are the people who most readily see the Black Panther Party as a means to change their lot in particular and the lot of the Black people in general. When these people come into the Party they bring these individualist tendencies with them. Within the Party these tendencies prevent Party policies from being carried out well or not at all. On the one hand, an individual trying to survive in the present society following only the rules and laws that serve you individually and rejecting those that do not is revolutionary by nature. On the other hand, coming into the Party and continuing to obey only orders and directions of the Party that please or satisfy you individually is counter-revolutionary and is called ultra-democracy. A few examples are: "the Panther Party should apply democratic centralism from the bottom to the top, or should let the lower levels discuss all problems first and then let the higher levels decide." On an individual level, a Panther was told by an officer to clean one of the Panther cars, and he responded by saying, "I don't drive the car; therefore I won't clean the car." This is ultra-democracy. If it is not eradicated it will damage or completely wreck the party organization. Some methods of correction are as follows: (a) Education of the rank and file to destroy the roots of ultra-democracy. (b) To ensure democracy under centralized guidance (1) the leadership must give correct guidance and solve problems when they arise in order to establish themselves as centers of leadership; (2) the leadership must know the life of the masses and be familiar with the situation in the rank and file in order to have an objective basis for correct guidance; (3) at no level in the Party should decisions be made casually in solving problems; (4) all major decisions and policies made by the leadership of the Party must be immediately communicated to the rank and file; (5) the rank and file must discuss decisions and policies of the leadership of the Party in order to understand them and decide on the methods of carrying them out.

17. African Patriotic Armed Struggle Grows In Strength February 17, 1969. Page 14

Only by persevering in armed struggle at home can any nation overthrow hated vicious colonial rule and win complete national independence and liberation. This is what the broad masses in the African countries, which have yet to achieve independence, have come to grasp profoundly in their protracted struggle against the enemy. In 1968, the patriotic armed forces of Guinea (Bissau), Mozambique, Angola, the Congo (Kinshasa) and Zimbabwe fought hundreds of battles with Portuguese colonial forces[,] Mobutu's puppet soldiers and the fascist troops of South Africa and Southern Rhodesia – all backed by imperialism headed by the United States. The patriotic armed forces enjoyed the support of the people and, by giving full play to courage in battle and surmounting one difficulty after another, wiped out several thousand enemy troops and extended their sphere of operations in a number of regions. This has greatly boosted the fighting will of the African people. As for the enemy troops, battered incessantly by the patriotic armed forces, morale sank lower and lower and the colonialists found the going in Africa tougher and tougher.

FREEDOM FIGHTERS GREAT Guinea (Bissau): Freedom fighters expand areas under control. In west Africa, the patriotic armed forces of Guinea (Bissau), fighting guns in hand for more than seven years, pressed on with their victories after having valiantly repulsed the attacks of the Portuguese colonial troops who tried to reoccupy the areas under their control. Beginning from June last year, they won a series of victories in repeated attacks on Portuguese colonial troops entrenched in a number of strongholds in the southern, northern and eastern parts of their country. By October, they had taken ten enemy encampments and strongholds, including Beli, capital city of the Boe region in the east. The Guinean (Bissau) patriotic armed forces shelled the airport in Bissau, the military and political centre of the Portuguese colonialists in the region, blasting the control tower and three hangars. Two enemy aircraft were destroyed and many damaged. The patriotic forces steadily expanded the areas under their control in the fighting. Apart from Bissau, Bolamo, dos Bijagos and areas on the northern seaboard, reports say, the rest of Guinea (Bissau) has at present virtually come under the control of the patriotic armed forces. Mozambique: Twelve enemy planes destroyed in one blow. Since their armed uprising in 1964, the patriotic armed forces of Mozambique in east Africa have long controlled vast areas in the two north-eastern Provinces of Niassa and Cabo Delgado. During the fighting in 1965, they wiped out more than 1,000 Portuguese colonial troops and extended the fighting from Cabo Delgado and Niassa Provinces to the mineral-rich province of Tete in the west. There they opened a new front and smashed attempts by the Portuguese colonialists to prevent the raging flames of the African people's armed struggle from spreading to the south. On August 10, 1968, the patriotic armed forces mounted an attack on the Portuguese air base in Mueda, destroying 12 enemy aircraft in one blow (see p. 20). Angola: Over 1,000 colonial troops wiped out in 4 months. The Angolan patriotic armed forces were the first to embark on the road of armed struggle in the Portuguese colonies in Africa. In 1968, they dealt telling blows to the Portuguese colonial troops in the vast eastern and northern areas. From July to October, they wiped out more than 1,000 enemy troops. Units active in the extensive rural areas of Mexico and Cuando Cubango Districts in the southeast and Lunda District in the northeast struck at the enemy incessantly. In the first four months of 1968, they put out of action 2500 Portuguese colonial troops and captured one Portuguese officer. Congo (K): Armed struggle heroically carried on. Subjected to ruthless suppression by U.S. imperialism and its lackey Mobutu and shamelessly betrayed by the Soviet revisionist renegade clique, the Congolese (K) patriotic forces heroically carried on their struggle. They recently raided a Mobutu Puppet military outpost in the Kwilu region, inflicting heavy losses on the enemy troops. Their courageous struggle nailed the lie spread by Mobutu, running dog of U.S. imperialism, that the Congolese(K) people's armed struggle has been put down. Southern Rhodesia: Colonial regime gripped by fear. The frequent operations of the Zimbabwean armed patriots have kept the Smith colonial regime in a state of continuous fear and panic. Shots fired by freedom fighters against South African colonial rule were also heard in South West Africa which is under the tight control of the South African White colonialists. The freedom fighters in South West Africa, reports say, killed 20 of the South African colonial troops in a recent battle.

LEARN WARFARE THROUGH WARFARE The African patriots learn warfare through warfare. Being constantly tempered in the crucible of fighting, their combat strength has increased and the level of their tactics raised steadily. In many areas, the patriotic armed forces have grown in strength, developing from small contingents of fighters carrying out hit-and-run harassment activities to the concentration of superior forces undertaking planned operations to wipe out enemy effectives. They often apply the tactics of inducing the enemy to go deep into their areas in order to attack and eliminate his troops. The war has educated the people and the people support the revolutionary war. Chairman Mao's brilliant thought -- the revolutionary war is a war of the masses -- has taken firm root in the minds of the people. More and more African patriots now realize that in their confrontation with the enemy, who is armed to the teeth and enjoys temporary numerical superiority, it is impossible to carry on protracted war or to win victory in the revolutionary war unless attention is paid to mobilizing and relying on the broad masses, particularly the peasant masses who constitute the overwhelming majority of the population in these countries. As it is, a number of African patriots have gone to the rural areas to rouse the masses. In Guinea (Bissau), Mozambique, Angola and the Congo(K), the patriotic armed forces have set up administrative organs in a number of areas under their control, and in some places they have their own law courts as well. They have also extensively organized militia forces in areas under the control. In some places, the militiamen participate in agricultural production and at the same time assume the duties of defending their villages. They are effective assistants of the guerrillas, serving as guides and messengers, furnishing information and transporting ammunition and supplies. In some areas, the African patriotic armed forces have helped the people raise their political consciousness by organizing the masses to recall national humiliation at the hands of the alien invaders and denounce the crime of colonial rule. In some areas, a number of African women have actively participated in patriotic activities, not only persuading their near and dear ones to go to the front but asking for permission to bear arms in the armed struggle. The African patriotic armed forces have also paid attention to increasing production, particularly that of grain, in the areas under their control, so that they can wage a protracted struggle by relying on their own resources. In some places, they have developed the educational and public health servicw[e]s. In the areas under their control, for instance, the Guinean (Bissau) patriots have abolished the exorbitant taxes and miscellaneous levies imposed on the people by the colonialists in the past and have opened up wasteland to develop production in a big way. As a result, rice and other grain output has increased and the handicraft industry has also developed. The guerrilla fighters in Mozambique make a point of working in the fields with the local peasants in areas they control. In some places, the Mozambique armymen and people are able to ship part of their farm produce to neighboring independent countries in exchange for clothing, medicine and other daily necessities. In the eastern part of Angola, the patriotic armed forces have set up peasant's mutual-aid and co-operative organizations and have trained a group of medical workers in areas under their control.

U.S. IMPERIALISM In their protracted war against colonialism, an increasing number of African people have begun to see things more clearly from their own experience and greatly raised their political consciousness. It is now clear to them that U.S. imperialism is their No. 1 enemy. Facts have made it abundantly clear that it is U.S. imperialism which has directed the Mobutu puppet clique to wantonly suppress the patriotic armed forces and people of the Congo (K). It is the same U.S. imperialism which gives vigorous support to the Portuguese colonialists in waging a barbarous war in Africa and tries to prop up their tottering colonial rule. And again it is the same U.S. imperialism which backs the white racist regimes in South Africa and Southern Rhodesia to slaughter the African people in cold Blood. These facts have laid bare still further the fiendish features of U.S. imperialism as the most ferocious enemy of the African people. The Soviet revisionist renegade clique, U.S. imperialism's No. 1 accomplice, has spread all kinds of revisionist fallacies far and wide in Africa, to cater to the needs of U.S. imperialism. It has tried to disintegrate the African patriotic armed forces by cajolery and bribery and to undermine the African people's patriotic armed struggle. It is common knowledge that over the years the Soviet revisionist renegade clique has been diabolically engaged in selling out the interest of the c[C]ongolese(K) and to murder Patrice Lumumba and S[s]trangle the legal Lumumba government. It advocates "reconciliation" between the Congolese(K) revolutionaries and the stooges of U.S.

imperialism, trying in a thousand and one ways to sabotage the Congolese people's patriotic armed struggle and split the national-liberation movement in the Congo(K). Recently, this clique "restored diplomatic relations" with the Mobutu puppet regime, U.S. imperialism's running dog and Lumumba's murderer, thus once again ignominiously betraying the Congolese(K) people's revolutionary cause. The lesson of the temporary reverses of the revolutionary cause in the Congo(K) is a characteristic illustration of the fact that the Soviet revisionist renegade clique is another most dangerous enemy of the African people. Therefore, in addition to opposing U.S. imperialism and its lackeys, the African people must wage a resolute struggle against the Soviet revisionist renegade clique in order to carry the revolution through to the end. It is precisely because the enemies confronting the revolutionary African people are not only the Portuguese, South African and Southern Rhodesian colonialists but also U.S. imperialism and the Soviet revisionist renegade clique, enemies who are far more vis[c]ious and cunning, that the African revolutionary people's struggle is protracted, arduous and at time tortuous. But as Chairman Mao, the great leader of the Chinese people, has wisely pointed out: "A nation, big or small, can defeat any enemy, however powerful, so long as it fully arouses its people, firmly relies on them and wage a people's war." We are convinced that the African people, who have a long tradition of struggle against imperialism and colonialism, will eventually crush imperialism, revisionism and all the reactionary forces, heavily weighing them down and win NATIONAL LIBERATION and complete emancipation.

18. The True Culture Of Africa And Africans
February 17, 1969. Pages 15-17

Patrice Lumumba, martyred leader of the revolutionary struggle in the Congo was a victim of capitalist inspired violence and terrorism in an attempt to stem the tide of the African Revolution. Lumumba is seated here in a jeep, hands bound, just prior to his assassination.

Today the revolutionary people of Congo (K), Mozambique, Angola, Guinea (Bissau), Zimbabwe and other places are carrying on life-and-death armed struggles against imperialism and its lackeys. Some of them have already established rural revolutionary base areas, while others are intensifying their armed activities and dealing powerful blows at the enemy. The Congo (K) declared its independence in 1960. U.S. imperialism, hand in glove with Soviet revisionism, hastily sent in U.S.-controlled aggressive armed forces under the flag of "The United Nations troops". The countless crimes of these aggressive troops include suppressing the patriotic forces, murdering the national hero Lumumba, subverting the legitimate government and installing a puppet regime. During those days of grave national disaster, patriotic armed forces of Kwilu in the western part of the Congo (K) kindled the fire of patriotic armed struggle against the U.S. imperialists and their puppets. Burning furiously, its flames spread to the northeastern and eastern parts of the country. While summing up their experiences and lessons in the last year and more, some leaders of the patriotic armed forces have come to realize the important significance of establishing a revolutionary political party, an army and a united front led by the revolutionary political party. Now, the patriotic armed forces have established revolutionary political power on the western front and expanded the struggle to the east and south of the base area. Since launching an armed uprising in September 1964, the people of Mozambique have set up active base areas in two northern provinces and launched a struggle in a province in the northwest. They make frequent attacks on isolated strongholds of the enemy while constantly ambushing enemy patrols. Since the beginning of this year, the freedom fighters have been consistently winning new victories. The Portuguese colonialist troops, badly beaten, are frightened to death. In Angola, the people have persisted in armed struggle for eight years. They have established some active base areas in the Cabinda area and in the eastern part of the country where they are now carrying on armed activities. In late February this year, guerrilla forces triumphantly smashed the Portuguese colonial army barracks at a certain place. The anti-imperialist armed struggle in Guinea (Bissau) started in 1961. Although the Portuguese colonialists, supported by U.S. imperialism, tried viciously to crush the local patriotic armed forces, the patriotic people, far from being suppressed, have resolutely continued to hold high the banner of armed struggle and are fighting on heroically. Their armed forces have liberated almost two-thirds of the country's territory. Moreover, constantly seizing the offensive, they have attacked Portuguese colonialist troops entrenched in a number of strongholds. Meanwhile in the territory under their own control, they have set up various mass fighting organizations, developed production and expanded cultural and educational activities. In April, 1966 the people of Zimbabwe also raise[d/s —illegible] high the banner of armed struggle. For the last two years and more they have been smashing the military "encirclement and suppression" campaigns waged by the Smith white colonialist authorities with the support of the British and U.S. imperialists. They have strengthened their own forces in the struggle. The raging flames of anti-imperialist struggle waged by the African people have now spread to South Africa. For example, since August 1966, the freedom fighters of Southwest Africa have engaged in vigorous armed resistance, killing many colonialist troops. So long as the broad masses of the African people, taking the road of armed struggle, maintain unity and persist in protracted struggle, no matter what the difficulties and hardships, they will surely drive imperialism and colonialism out of Africa.

Eliel Paul Mwaluko, Ambassador of the United Republic of Tanzania to China, gave a reception in Peking on January 11, to mark the 5th anniversary of the Zanzibar Revolution. Present on the occasion were Kuo Mo-jo, Vice-Chairman of the National People's Congress, and leading members of the government department concerned and of the Peking Municipal Revolutionary Committee. In his speech at the reception, Ambassador Mwaluko described the significance of the Zanzibar people's armed revolution and their achievements in construction after the victory of the revolution. The Ambassador warmly greeted the success of China's new hydrogen bomb test. He said: This great victory is a fruitful result of the great proletarian cultural revolution being carried out under the wise leadership of Chairman Mao. We rejoice over China's victories and achievements just as if they are our own. Speaking of China's aid to his country, the Ambassador said: The sincere aid provided by China to Tanzania has increased our revolutionary courage and confidence. We are very grateful to Chairman Mao and the Chinese Government. Vice-Minister of Foreign Affairs Chi Peng-fei, in his speech, paid tribute to the Zanzibar people who bravely took up arms and waged an armed struggle to oppose the reactionary rule of imperialism and its running dogs and finally won national independence. He also paid tribute to the Tanzanian people who, under the leadership of President Nyerere, have in the past five years scored one achievement after another in the struggle to safe-guard national independence and in building their country. Chi Peng-fei added: The great leader of the Chinese people Chairman Mao has pointed out: "The world revolution has entered a great new era." We are deeply convinced that in this new year, the people of Tanzania and other countries in Africa will win new victories in their anti-imperialist struggles, and that there will be a new development in the friendly relations between the Chinese and Tanzanian peoples.

19. Fifth Anniversary Of The Zanzibar Revolution. February 17, 1969. Page 17

Eliel Paul Mwaluko, Ambassador of the United Republic of Tanzania to China, gave a reception to Peking on January 11, to mark the fifth anniversary of the Zanzibar Revolution. Present on the occasion were Kuo Mo-jo, Vice-Chairman of the Standing Committee of the National People's Congress, and leading members of the government department concerned, and of the Peking Municipal Revolutionary Committee. In his speech at the reception, Ambassador Mwaluko described the significance of the Zanzibar people's armed revolution and their achievements in construction after the victory of the revolution. The Ambassador warmly greeted the success of China's new hydrogen bomb test. He said: "This great victory is a fruitful result of the great proletarian cultural revolution being carried out under the wise leadership of Chairman Mao. We rejoice over China's victories and achievements just as if they are our own ." Speaking of China's aid to his country, the Ambassador said: "The sincere aid provided by China to Tanzania has increased our revolutionary courage and confidence. We are very grateful to Chairman Mao and the Chinese Government." Vice-Minister of Foreign Affairs Chi Peng-fei, in his speech, paid tribute to the Zanzibar people who bravely took up arms and waged an armed struggle to oppose the reactionary role of imperialism and its running dogs and finally won national independence . He also paid tribute to the Tanzanian people who, under the leadership of President Nyerere, have in the past five years scored one achievement after another in the struggle to safeguard national independence and in building their country. Chi Peng-fei added: "The great leader of the Chinese people, Chairman Mao, has pointed out: 'The world revolution has entered a great new era.' We are deeply convinced that in this new year, the people of Tanzania and other countries in Africa will win new victories in their anti-imperialist struggles, and that there will be a new development in the friendly relations between the Chinese and Tanzanian peoples.

20. MESSAGE FROM HUEY MARCH 3, 1969.
PAGE 2. TAPED IN PRISON. HUEY P. NEWTON,
MINISTER OF DEFENSE, BLACK PANTHER PARTY

REVOLUTIONARY BROTHERS AND SISTERS, WHITE RADI-
CALS WHO ARE BECOMING BROTHERS AND SISTERS: I'm very
happy that we are all here together today, not because it's
my birthday, but because we should be together on any and
every occasion that we possibly can in the name of solidarity. February 17th, fortunately, is also the Tet of the lunar
new year. So we're celebrating the lunar new year with our
brothers in Viet Nam. We're daily making the people more
and more aware of the need for unity among all revolutionary people and also that it's impossible for us to overcome
the treacherous bureaucratic class without an organized force.
The students at the many universities across the nation are
challenging the reactionary authority of the schools and are
also pointing out very vividly that it's impossible to have a
free university, free schools, or a free society in a society that's
ruled by a fascist military-industrial complex. The community is now seeing that our fight on the campuses is more
than just a fight for "freedom of speech" on the campus, or
Blacks gaining a knowledge of our heritage; it's also show-

ing the direct relationship between the reactionary government and the agencies and institutions that are only an arm of these reactionaries. Until we penetrate the community and make them aware and plant the seed of revolution, we will never have freedom at our schools. The community now is being mobilized by the Black revolutionary forces and along with them are our white revolutionary comrades. It seems that the time has come for an escalation of our offensive. Just as our brothers in Viet Nam had the Tet offensive last year, this celebration today will only be a prelude or celebration to the offensive that we are going to wage in the not-too-far future. "In the near future a colossal event will occur where the masses of the people will rise up like a mighty storm and a hurricane, sweeping all evil gentry and corrupt officials into their graves." Brother Mao put that quite well, and we will follow the pattern and follow the thoughts of Chairman Mao. Today it should mark a new time for the two-revolutionary force in the country (the two-revolutionary force I'm speaking of is the alienated white group and the masses of Blacks in the ghettos, who for years sought freedom and liberation from a racist, reaction system). After approximately three years now that the Panthers have been organized, we have gained an even closer relationship with our Latin American brothers, our Chicano brothers in the United States, the Cuban people, and every other people who are striving for freedom. I would like to thank everyone very much for coming and we must remember that we must never make excuses for such gatherings as this. Today we'll use the excuse of my birthday; but the real issue is the need to come together in unity and brotherhood. Our Minister of Information, Eldridge Cleaver, is with us in spirit and I'm very sure that this decadent fascist society wasn't worthy of him and couldn't tolerate his presence because he acted as a guide flag for the people. So we must make a society that will welcome people like our Minister of Information. The Oakland Seven are now standing trial for resisting the fascist system, and we would like to let them know and would like to rally the community for support. They have a very able representative in court with them, Charles Garry, who is very capable and truly a revolutionary. Brother Eldridge Cleaver has said on more than one occasion that he would go into any court in the world with an attorney like Charles Garry. I would like to bear witness to that from a personal experience. With a representative like Charles Garry we're sure that we would have victory as long as the community supports us. We have, with the support of the community and with the fine attorney such as Charles Garry, we have nothing to fear. A short time ago we suffered a very tragic experience in that two of our very talented and gifted and dedicated brothers were assassinated in Los Angeles: Brother "Bunchy" and Brother Huggins. This was only an escalation of the oppression against us. The assassins were agents of the establishment and they took the occasion to eliminate the people's fighters, or fighters for the people. Knowing that the people have no recourse, the institutions and the court institutions give us no recourse because they're only representatives of the reactionary system. The community will have to erect revolutionary courts and also a community militia to protect the community and see that the community gets justice. Brother Ruben has suffered many investigations, and now he's under investigation. He's going to trial on or about four or five different alleged crimes, and the crimes are seeking justice. The society views any person who's striving after justice and freedom and to end exploitation as a "criminal." We know that if we are criminals, the criminals have received their ultimate revenge when Karl Marx indicted the bourgeoisie of grand theft. We realize that it's they who are criminals and it's they who will have to be brought to justice. We will have to go on fighting in spite of the losses and in spite of the hardships that we're bound to suffer, until the final downfall of the reactionary power structure. So, power to the people, black power to black people, and panther power to the vanguard!

21. COLOMBIAN PEOPLE'S LIBERATION ARMY
REVOLUTION, MARCH 3, 1969. PAGE 6

Organ of the Colombian Communist Party (Marxist-Leninist), recently published a document which pointed out the tremendous achievements in the first year of the revolutionary armed struggle unfolded by the Colombian People's Liberation Army, and called upon the revolutionary people of Colombia to strengthen their struggles and strike hard at U. S. imperialism and the Columbian oligarchies. The document was jointly issued by the Colombian Communist Party (Marxist-Leninist), the People's Liberation Army and the Regional Patriotic Committee of Alto Sino and Alto San Jorge.

It pointed out first of all that the broad masses of the Colombian people are rising up in struggle in all parts of the country and their political consciousness is rapidly heightening. It said: "Standing in the forefront of the triumphant struggle of the Colombian people is the Colombian Communist Party (Marxist-Leninist)." In Colombia, "the People's Liberation Army, the armed arm of our Party, has emerged and has been growing stronger daily. Today, it has become the brain and spine of the armed struggle of our people. "The People's Liberation Army," it continued, "has unfolded its struggle on three principal fronts: fighting the enemy; undertaking and developing production; and mobilizing, educating, organizing and arming the broad masses of the people. Our people's army is fighting under the slogans of 'absolute confidence in victory, profound and boundless love for our people and irreconcilable hatred for our class enemies.' We are convinced that 'we are bound to win the fight.'" The document said: "Parallel to the People's Liberation Army, there have appeared the revolutionary peasant militia and the regional patriotic committees. The last-mentioned are the embryo of a patriotic front for liberation." It pointed out: "The People's Liberation Army replied to the suppression of U. S. Imperialism and the operations in the first year beginning from June 1967. In the first year's combats, the People's Liberation Army killed or wounded many enemy soldiers, captured a number of weapons and recovered the U.S. imperialist enterprises and from the oligarchies hundreds of thousands of pesos worth of goods. It also recovered several thousand hectares of land and thousands of cattle and horses from the hands of the big latifundists. In the course of fighting, 'the People's Liberation Army has forged ahead in its development and its combat determination has brought about great success. These successes have strengthened our people's confidence in and profound love for their own armed forces.'" The document condemned the reactionary authorities for cruelly persecuting the peaceable inhabitants. It stated: "The Colombian Communist Party (Marxist-Leninist), the People's Liberation Army and the patriotic committees, carrying out the line of the Party and applying the thought of the great teacher Comrade Mao Tse-tung, shall continue to stand at the head of the people and point out to them the road of revolution." It called on the Colombian people to counter with conscious struggles the repression, oppression and exploitation of the people by U. S. imperialism and the Colombian oligarchies and to firmly support the People's Liberation Army. It also called on all the fighters of the People's Liberation Army and revolutionary peasant militia to redouble their efforts in annihilating the enemy.

Revolution has also published war communique No. 9 of the People's Liberation Army which reported the combat achievements of the People's Liberation Army in June and July, 1968. The communique pointed out that the People's Liberation Army has grown stron ger in the course of fighting. In the first eight months of fighting, eight detachments were set up, including the "Maria Cano" detachment composed of women fighters.

22. WASHINGTON/MOSCOW COLLABORATION INTENSIFIED MARCH 3, 1969. PAGE 8.

Shortly before and immediately after Nixon took office, the renegades in the Kremlin went out of their way, openly and covertly, to flatter and toady to the new boss of the U. S. imperialism. Impatient to establish connections with the new set-up of the American monopoly capitalist class, they engaged in wide-scale diplomacy behind the scenes in Washington, New York and other American cities. They even sent a delegation of what they called "public leaders" to the United States to "exchange opinions on Soviet-American relations and a number of current international problems." In their own words, all this represents "joint efforts . . . to solve the ripe international problems" with U. S. imperialism. Even Western reporters were "surprised" by the Soviet revisionist renegade clique's feverish anxiety to do business with U. S. imperialism at the first opportunity. The British paper *Evening Standard* published a Washington report on January 29, saying: "Soviet diplomats, it is now known, contacted members of the Nixon staff in New York shortly before the inauguration and extended talks took place with Henry Kissinger, Nixon's White House adviser on foreign policy. And over the last few days Georgi Zhukov, the political commentator of *Pravda* ... has been in Washington for quiet talks with key members of Congress." The paper added: "The pace and urgency of the Soviet approaches have surprised most experts here." It quoted a U. S. official as saying, "It's so promising ... I've never known them to be in this much of a hurry." The nauseating fawning on the new U. S. imperialist chieftain by the clique of Soviet revisionist renegades and their impatience to fraternize with U. S. imperialism are not only a new exposure of their true colors as renegades but also a confession of their difficulties and dire plight both at home and abroad.

U. S. imperialism quite appreciates the way the Soviet revisionist renegades dance to its tune. *U.S. News And World Report*, a U. S. monopoly capital mouthpiece said, "High on the Nixon agenda is the search for better relations with Russia." One of the important items in the further counter-revolutionary global deals between the United States and the Soviet Union now under preparation is the so-called limitation of nuclear missiles. As a "gift" to Nixon on the day of his inauguration, the Soviet revisionist renegade clique made a "proposal" on this question to U. S. State Department spokesman McCloskey declared that U. S. imperialism "is giving priority consideration to the question of beginning talks" with the Soviet revisionists. Nixon himself made it clearer still on January 27 at his first press conference after assuming office that talks on this question were only the beginning of a series of counter-revolutionary global deals between the two countries. He said: "What I want to do is to see to it that we have strategic arms talks in a way and at a time that will promote, if possible, progress on outstanding political problems at the same time." Western news agencies pointed out that Nixon's statement showed he was ready to have "a broad dialogue" with the Soviet revisionists and he hoped this could gradually lead to "concerted efforts" by the U. S. imperialism and Soviet revisionism "on a scale never previously achieved." At his February 6 press conference, Nixon indicated that the United States agreed to the recent proposal repeatedly put forward by the Soviet revisionists that representatives of the United States, the Soviet Union, Britain and France should hold meetings at the United Nations to discuss a so-called "political solution" to the Middle East problem. He stressed that "initiative" on the problem "must be multilateral." This means U. S. imperialism wants the four countries to take "joint action" to put pressure on the Arab people and compel them to swallow a fraudulent "political solution." Nixon again dropped the hint to the Soviet revisionists that if they wanted to clinch the deal with the United States on the "limitation" of the missile race, they must collaborate still further with the United States regarding a settlement of the Middle East problem, that is, they must join the United States in efforts to stifle the just struggle of the Arab people, the armed struggle of the Palestinian people in particular. In response to the call by Nixon for an "open society," the Soviet revisionists have granted permission to the U. S. Overseas National Airways to operate 20 chartered flights between New York and Leningrad for 1969, beginning from March. Each flight will bring 200 American "tourists" to the Soviet Union to spread malodorous bourgeois influence among the Soviet people. For its part, the Soviet revisionism sent delegation after delegation to the United States in "exchange." It is also quietly agreed to send an "observer" to a conference on the "communications satellite system" in Washington this month. This means that the Soviet revisionists will join the U. S. imperialists in the dirty activities of collecting information. During this intensified collaboration that was being worked out between U. S. imperialism and Soviet revisionism, U.S. NEWS AND WORLD REPORT, in a recent article, divulged the criminal objective of U. S. imperialism and Soviet revisionism, the two most ferocious enemies of the revolutionary people of the world, which are collaborating and struggling with each other in their vain effort to re-divide the world between themselves. It said: "What the Kremlin wants from Mr. Nixon is an agreement that the U.S. and Russia should get together and divide the world into spheres of interest and influence, with a few "no man's lands" open for grabs. The more U.S. imperialism and Soviet revisionism intensify their collusion, the more clearly will they reveal their ferocious features before the people of the world and the more quickly will they go to their doom.

23. Cultural Nationalism Attacked In Emory Douglas Speech. March, 1969

This article is a reprint from Western Front newspaper -- Washington State Peace and Freedom Party. By Calvin Winslow Bobby Seale, Chairman of the Black Panther Party, was scheduled to speak February 1, at the Encore Ballroom. That afternoon the Panthers announced that Seale would not be able to make it to Seattle. Those who passed up the meeting, however, made a mistake. Emory Douglas, Minister of Culture of the BPP, stood in for Seale and proved once again that the leadership of the BPP includes many of the most articulate, dedicated revolutionaries of our time. The central issue raised in the meeting, discussed by both Douglas and Aaron Dixon, Seattle Panther Captain, was the recent assassination in Los Angeles of Alprentice Carter and John Huggins, L.A. Panther leaders. The Panthers have accused US, a cultural nationalist organization led by Ron Karenga, of killing "two beautiful black brothers in the prime of revolutionary life of serving our people."

US, based in Watts, has put forth the idea of uniting all black people, regardless of class or ideology, while at the same time accepting federal money and promoting black capitalism. That cultural nationalism has now become so blatantly counter-revolutionary should not be surprising. Huey Newton pointed out some time ago that blacks can easily be used by the state to oppress their brothers. US has now turned its guns on the Panthers. This must certainly be another indication that the United States government spends its money carefully--the system can find its real enemies. In declaring their opposition to cultural nationalism, the Panthers have increased the number of their enemies, but far more importantly, they have also rededicated themselves to serving the real interests of the people. Poor people need political power, not Dashikis. Black capitalism will not free black people. It is capitalism which has made them poor. Emory Douglas said the Panthers will continue to organize the black community on a revolutionary basis. "The whole of Westwood (part of white Los Angeles, where UCLA is located and where the two Panthers were assassinated)," he added, "is not worth a few organized blocks of the Oakland flatlands." The Panthers now have over 80 branches, and from each an ultimatum has been issued warning Karenga and his followers to stay away. Dixon added that Seattle was included. For those who are still looking forward to hearing Bobby Seale, Dixon said that the Panthers plan to bring him to Seattle in the near future. Watch for the time.

24. SOUTHWEST AFRICA FOLLOWS CHAIRMAN MAO. MARCH 16, 1969. PAGES 12-13

"The oppressed peoples and nations must not pin their hopes for liberation on the "sensibleness" of imperialism and its lackeys. They will only triumph by strengthening their unity and persevering in their struggle." This quotation from Chairman Mao shows us, the South West African people, the correct path for our liberation. It is erroneous to pin our hopes for liberation on the "sensibleness" of the United Nations which is controlled by the U.S. imperialists and their accomplices the Kruschchov revisionists of the Soviet Union.

A BRIEF HISTORICAL BACKGROUND Under the pretext of protecting the "interests" of a German "Merchant" one Luderitz, and with the connivance of British imperialism, which had vast colonial possessions in the Territory, German imperialism finally effected the colonialization of South West Africa in 1884. Increasing numbers of German colonial troops were brought into the Territory. Our people rose in a war of Resistance to German savagery, which reached explosive proportions in the period between 1903-1907. South West Africa remained a German colonial possession until after the beginning of the First World War. On July, 1915, the South

African colonial troops undertook the conquest of South West Africa. The First World War was over. The "Mandate System", in regard to former German colonies and the League of Nations became some of the products of the "Peace Settlements". Woodrow Wilson of the United states was instrumental in the creation of the "Mandate system". The League of Nations "mandate" was signed in Geneva on December 17, 1920. The British Government, on whom the "mandate" was originally conferred upon, agreed without hesitation that the "mandate" be exercised on her behalf by the South African colonial authorities. The people of South West Africa were neither asked nor consulted. It was merely a division of the booty between old and new oppressors. The heinous crime was committed in the name of "the material and moral well-being and the social progress" of the people of South West Africa and under the guise of "international supervision". Then came the Second World War. Our people were drafted into the armies of the countries of the anti-Hitler coalition. They were made to believe that they were fighting for "democracy" and "freedom" throughout the world. The declarations at San Francisco strengthened these false impressions. After the War our people found themselves back into the old position: slaves of oppressive white South Africa and Victims of imperialist treachery. It became very clear as time went on that the imperialist world and the United Nations were more concerned with the question of the balance of world forces which, as a consequence of the outcome of the Second World War, became unfavourable to international imperialism than with the emancipation of colonial peoples. A "dispute" them[n] arose between the United Nations and South Africa on whether the "Mandate" was still in existence, and that the United Nations had succeeded to the "supervisory" functions formally exercised by the counter-revolutionary League of Nations in respect of South West Africa. This was essentially due to the demands of some Afro-Asian and other friendly nations. For reasons better known to those who regarded themselves as champions of the cause of the people of South West Africa than the people of South West Africa themselves, this show which was given the label of a "dispute" was taken to the proimperialist International Court of Justice, which, as expected, ruled that South Africa's tyrannical rule over South West Africa should continue. Again our people were neither asked nor consulted. The events before and after the "ruling" of the Court clearly showed that the high-sounding legal platitudes were merely a cover to provide an appropriate opportunity for different interest-groupings which hold identical positions to hatch schemes against the interests of the South West African People and their movement for political liberation and social emancipation. In another futile attempt to mislead the awakening people of South West Africa, Africa and the whole world into the belief that the international counter-revolutionaries can liberate the people of South West Africa, U.S. imperialism ordered the United Nations to pass a fraudulent resolution "terminating" South Africa's rule over South West Africa. It was further alleged that the United Nations was assuming a direct "responsibility" over South West Africa. This nonsense was uttered on the 29th of Octov[b]er 1966 and May 1967 respectively. As a result of political squabbles in the United Nations, a so-called Council for South West Africa was manufactured to make this propaganda more believable. But one may ask: What is the purpose of declaring that the people of South West Africa were now free from South African rule in 1966 when, in fact, they remain ruled by South Africa in September 1968? This only helps to further reveal the hypocrisy of those who style themselves as our saviou[r]s. The so-called Council for South West Africa is merely engaged in endless demo[a]gogy, tourist-excursions and flagrant and irresponsible interference in South West Africa's internal affairs. Our people are carefully watching the activities of this group and its creators. What has neither failed to escape our attention are the activities of the Khrushchovites without Khrushchov on the question of South West Africa. They deliberately cover up the fact that the imperialists are already in South West Africa. In fact, they themselves are labouring, body and soul, together with U.S. imperialism to "enhance the role of the United Nations".

A QUOTATION FROM CHAIRMAN MAO TSE-TUNG: "They (die-hards) always have many schemes in hand, schemes for profiting at others' expense, for double-dealing, and so on. But they always get the opposite of what they want. They invariably start by doing others harm but end by ruining themselves."

The German philosopher Feuerbach said that those who try to comfort the slaves instead of arousing them to revolt against slavery are helping the slaveowners.

U.N. CAN NOT LIBERATE SOUTH WEST AFRICA Innumerable historical events (Congo(K), Korea, Palestine, for example) clearly shows that, the United Nations has degenerated into a tool of imperialist aggression whenever the interests of imperialism are at stake, and into a toothless bulldog when the cause of justice and freedom is menaced by the imperialist

92

hawks. It must be clearly understood that the actions of U.S. imperialism on the question of South West Africa are not only motivated by political considerations alone, but by economic reasons as well. American capital investment in South West Africa and other related economic interests must not be looked at in isolation from the entire political and economic position of the imperialist world in the whole of southern Africa. It is common knowledge that the social roots of apartheid are invariable[y] found in the imperialist economic system. Consequently, appeals for "an international force" from international capitalism will do us no good. But as the struggle for mineral wealth between various imperialist countries would continue, the U.S. imperialists are bent on finding ways of putting South West Africa under their direct domination. This would merely be a dog-eat-dog fight and should in no way be seen as a battle to liberate the people of South West Africa. After all how can those who oppress the Vietnamese people, the people of the Dominican Republic, the people of the whole world all of a sudden become so magnanimous in our case?

REVOLUTION DEPENDS ON MAO TSE-TUNG'S THOUGHT We in Swanu shall go our own way, we shall handle our affairs in our own fashion. While we do claim that everything is good with us, and it is possible that we have many shortcomings, we remain firm in our conviction that it is only the people of South West Africa alone who must liberate themselves; it is only the strategy and tactics of People's War formulated by Chairman Mao Tse-Tung and creatively applied to the concrete practice of the South West African Revolution that would lead our people along the road of genuine national liberation. We sincerely believe that this is the only correct road for our people to take. Consequently, we hold the view that a distinction must be made between a genuine guerrilla warfare anchored in the masses and the actions of a group of people forced by the thier leaders to "go back home and fight" in order to create a bait for collecting dollars and roubles abroad.

A QUOTATION FROM CHAIRMAN MAO TSE-TUNG: "The revolutionary war is a war of the masses; it can be waged only by mobilizing the masses and relying on them." Whatever our own difficulties, we honestly believe that without mobilizing the broad masses of the people, primarily the people in the country-side, establishing revolutionary base areas and following the strategy of encircling the cities from the country-side, neither big parades of "trainees" abroad, vagabond mentality nor the actions of a few people can push the cause of our people forward. Recent developments in South West Africa and some other Latin American and African countries clearly speak for themselves. We in the South West Africa National Union believe that our difficulties are temporary and that a bright future is lying ahead of us, however long that may take. Chairman Mao has taught us: "The reactionary forces and we both have difficulties. But the difficulties of the reactionary forces are insurmountable because they are forces on the verge of death and have no future. Our difficulties can be overcome because we are new and rising force and have a bright future."

FINAL VICTORY BELONGS TO THE PEOPLE OF SOUTH WEST AFRICA DARING TO STRUGGLE AND DARING TO WIN!

All Power to the People

25. U.S. Imperialism Is Dying March 16, 1969. Page 15.

U. S. imperialism is intensifying fascistization at home. Tightening the machinery of the dictatorship of the bourgeoisie with redoubled efforts, it is subjecting the American people to a reign of terror and bloody suppression that is worse than before and has turned the United States into a huge prison. Chairman Mao pointed out in 1949: "The governments of Hitler, Mussolini, Tojo, Franco and Chiang Kai-shek discarded the veil of democracy for the bourgeoisie or never used it because the class struggle in their countries was extremely intense and they found it advantageous to discard, or not to use, this veil lest the people too should make use of it." Chairman Mao also predicted at the time that the U. S. imperialism would inevitably follow the same road. Events have turned out exactly this way!

Since the end of World War II, U. S. imperialism has been playing the role of "international gendarme" in frantically suppressing the people of many countries. But inside the United States it has tried hard to put on an air of respectability by hiding its ruthless rule behind a veil of "democracy." However, with the daily sharpening of the class struggle in the country, this veil has long been torn to shreds by U. S.

ruling circles themselves. U. S. imperialism is now stepping up its fascistization and making savage onslaughts on the people. This completely reveals its ferocious features. The intensified fascistization by U. S. ruling circles reflects the rapid exacerbation of the political-economic crisis of U. S. imperialism, the inevitable result of the rapid and vigorous development of the American people's revolutionary struggle. Like roaring waves, the struggle of the Black Americans against racial oppression, the workers' movement and the student movement have violently pounded the reactionary rule of the U. S. monopoly capitalists in recent years. Since deception and trickery have failed to stop the tempestuous torrents, U. S. ruling circles are banking on the bayonet to maintain their rule. Thus the intensified fascist dictatorship at home by

U. S. imperialism is by no means a sign of strength. It only betrays its weakness. It is a sign of U.

S. imperialism nearing the end of its rope. Fascism is itself the product of the imperialist system in decline. Once fascism is introduced it inevitably accelerates the collapse of this system. Outright violence under the savage rule of the

U. S. imperialists will only disabuse the masses of much of their illusions about bourgeois democracy and help bring about a greater awakening of the American people. It will help them see more clearly that only by using revolutionary violence against counter-revolutionary violence can genuine emancipation be achieved. Fascist dictatorship, far from destroying the revolutionary movement of the American people, will only create powerful grave-diggers of U. S. imperialism. Fascism did not save Hitler from destruction. Neither can it save U. S. imperialism from its final doom!

26. BLACK CAPITALISM AND WHAT IT MEANS.
MARCH 23, 1969. PAGES 2-3.
BY LANDON WILLIAMS

While reading the paper the other day, I saw where Oakland has been made a target area for tricky Dick Nixon's Black Capitalism Plan. It seems to me that a further analysis of capitalism in general and black capitalism in particular seems to be forthcoming. (When we check the history of various countries on this planet we find that many nations and races have gone through a capitalistic bag. When we check Russian history we find that with the ending of the rule of the Czar, Russian capitalism came to an end. When we check the history of China and yellow capitalism we find that with the coming to power of Mao Tse-tung and the communist party of China, that feudalism and bureaucratic capitalism to which the yellow people in China were subjected had been crushed. When we check the history of other countries that have gone capitalistic, such as India and brown capitalism, we find that today India is in a constant state of turmoil. I think that in viewing capitalist countries we should take into consideration the basic drives, motivations and the fundamental reasons for the things that occur in capitalistic countries. For instance, in checking the economy we find that in capitalistic countries a high unemployment rate, sometimes 10%-15%, is not something spectacular, but rather that in order for a capitalist country to maintain a balanced economy this type of unemployment rate is essential as a check on inflation. In further checking on capitalism and how it is related to black people in this country, if we want to find out what capitalism has in store for us all we have to do is look around and dig on our present situation because the conditions that black people are in[,] in this country is directly due to capitalism and the exploitation that we have suffered at the hands of the racist capitalist ruling classes here in racist America. We find that during the days of the slave trade, capitalist merchants along this country's Eastern seaboard got filthy rich off of the blood, the tears and the sweat of black people who were transported in the bottoms of ships, packed like sardines, to this racist decadent country to work and slave and die in the fields to build this country. Capitalism, as we all know, in order to exist, must have something or someone to exploit. What we have here in America is super capitalism, super exploitation; trinkets and heads are being sold to the people for exorbitantly high prices. In dealing with black capitalism or the little of it that we have experienced in this country by checking J. A. Rogers 100 AMAZING FACE ABOUT THE NEGRO we find that prior to the civil war there were small black capitalists in this country. These black capitalists to a certain extent enjoyed some of the benefits and privileges of this country insofar as they were called freemen and as such they could own slaves and property. In checking through history we find that most of these freedmen or miniature black capitalists had no concern or feeling whatsoever for the rest of their black brothers and sisters and in many instances they were more brutal than the white slavemasters and blamed their brothers for keeping them from enjoying all the fruits of the white capitalist class. During the civil war when the North and the South supposedly fought to free the slaves we find that some of these black capitalists in fact fought on the side of the confederacy to help maintain the exploitation over their black brothers. So when black people begin to see words such as capitalism it should appall them. You see, we've been trained in this country so that whenever we see the word communist, for instance, most black people will be startled but yet they see the word capitalism and it more or less doesn't phase them at all. They just continue on, it's just an everyday word, it's something that they've come up around. But I think that if black people would stop and really check out that word "capitalism" and what capitalism means on an every day basis, they would begin to be appalled by the word. Myself, when I saw this thing, "Oakland" being "in on black capitalism", to me that was a very[,] very terrifying thing because like I've said we've had examples of what capitalism has done. Black people in this country must begin to form the correct concepts in their minds when they hear the word capitalism. In this country, in schools, the little training they do give us when they deal with America or capitalism, they deals with democratic capitalism and they teach you about the democracy and not about the capitalism. The results are that when black people see the words "Oakland is in on black capitalism" immediately stanzas of the star spangled banner begin to play through their hands and they see the flag waving when what they should be seeing is the napalming of people of color in Viet Nam and the murder of Che Guevara in Bolivia by racist U.S., C.I.A. agents. Also when we think about capitalism we should think about our brothers and sisters in the Congo. There's a pamphlet called *Revolution In The Congo* which every black person in America should read and you will find out how capitalism operates. For instance when the U.S. intervened in the Congo and Patrice Lumumba, the people's choice for Premier, was murdered by that traitorous dog Tshombe who was a running dog for the U.S. and Belgian capitalists, and that jive liberal Kennedy. At the time of the U.S. intervention there were large copper mines in Katanga and other provinces in the Congo. There's a firm in the U.S. called Kennecut mines and they control most of the world's supply of copper. Well, at the time of the Congo intervention the supply of copper had begun to outstrip the demand and the price of copper had begun to drop. Well, these capitalists who sit up and control Chase Manhattan Bank and other large banks and industries made millions selling excess U.S. 10,000 lb. bombs to bomb the mining industry and the people of the Congo into rubble, thus beating down the competition. In America today the capitalist businessman and landlord exploits you at the store and home and then at the same time he goes to church and kneels his big hypocritical pork chop ass down and talks about brotherhood and do unte others as you would have them do unto you. And when you ask him how does he justify the cutthroat business practices he indulges in, he gives you the simple phrase that business is business. Well, I think we should take a very close look at just what is capitalist business. As I said, in the Congo it consists of dropping 10,000 lb. bombs on black people there. Prior to W.W. II the capitalist in this country who ran the junk yards were making millions of dollars by selling scrap iron and steel to the Japanese imperialists who were waging an unjust war of aggression against the Chinese people. Public opinion was very much against this practice. But again the excuse, "business is business" was used. In the realm of competition the capitalist in this country moves in many ways. With the onset of W.W. II thousands of our yellow brothers were incarcerated in so-called detention camps which were nothing but concentration camps. The reason given for their imprisonment: they were a security threat but rather [it was] American racism and American capitalism. The racism was clearly shown by the fact that hundreds of thousands of German and Italian nationals were not incarcerated but were instead allowed to run free to sabotage America's war effort. The Japanese at that time owned considerable rice lands in California; in fact they had the entire rice trade uptight. We find however that when they were moved on they were forced to sell out at ridiculous prices and in many cases their land was just taken from them -- again, business is business. So you can see that they were incarcerated for racist motives and capitalist motives. Going back further and checking out the history of this country we find that after the civil war was over black people in this country were promised forty acres and two mules by the Freedman's Bureau. When we check through history we find out just who got the forty acres and two mules. When we check we find that the large capitalist industries such as Standard Oil got the land. Standard Oil got my forty acres and my two mules. To them though this was just business. Again the massacre of the Indians or Manifest Destiny, that the white man glorifies on TV, was nothing but "business is business."

The white capitalist in this country, the mining industries, the oil companies, and the land barons who expected to set up their own small kingdoms, these warlords in America in order to gain more land would instigate incidents with the Indians so that they could call in the U. S. cavalry and Army and thereby rob the Indians of more land, the reason again given us was that "business is business." So that cutthroat competition and that steady drive for self-attainment and personal satisfaction that is preached in capitalist countries, Black people must begin to understand what it's all about. When we go down to the corner store and we find that we're being charged the highest prices for the lowest grades of meat and in many instances the meat is old and rotten. We should begin to form concepts of what capitalism means in a for real, day-to-day basis. Black people run up against this every day. What has capitalism meant to the vast majority of the peoples of the world? I think that is a question we should be asking ourselves. When we look around we find that the countries where the capitalist in America get most of their resources from, these colonies and semi-colonies that are called the underdeveloped countries of the world. When we look at them we find that there they have the highest infant mortality and death rates in the world and the lowest standards of living. Why is it likes that? Black people cannot accept what our enemy tells us as being all inclusive. Malcolm X said that if you had to rely on your enemy for a job you were in bad shape. It also holds true that if you have to rely on your enemy for information you're in bad shape. Black people must begin to form the proper concepts of just what capitalism is and just what it's all about so that they can begin to deal with the situation in the correct way. We find, again in checking history, that when capitalists move they move in very devilish, underhanded ways in order to control and manipulate the governments and the people throughout the world. In taking again the example of he Congo they used their favorite gimmick, the phony communist conspiracy type plot, and they said that Lumumba was a pro-communist and that Tshombe was pro-West. Again this is just a trick, a guise or deception that the capitalists use to cover up their filthy underhanded dealings. In China it was the same thing. When the U.S. was supporting the pirate Chiang Kai-shek's regime, they said that Chairman Mao Tse-tung was pro-communist and that Chiang Kai-shek was pro-West. At that time black people in this country generally accepted that without looking into it further and seeing just what did it mean to the pro-communist or pro-West. On deeper examination of the facts we find that the pirate Chiang Kai-shek who was pro-West was also pro-capitalist and pro-exploitation, while Mao Tse-Tung who was pro-communist was pro the people and pro-peasants. On the one hand you had Chiang Kai-shek who robbed from the people and was a tool that U.S. imperialism used to help maintain its dominance and exploitation over the Chinese people while Chairman Mao and the communist party of China were fighting for people, power and an end to the exploitation of the people. We see this same trick today in the news q[w]hen J. Edgar Hoover says that the Black Panther Party is a threat to the security of the U.S. and that we study from the Red Book and that we are pro-communist -- just what kind of threat did he mean and what is the Red Book? On examination we find that the primary objective of the Black Panther Party is "To establish revolutionary political power for black people." And that among the principles we study in the red book are such principles as "without a people's army the people have nothing." Huey P. Newton our founder and Minister of Defense has said, "A people who are unarmed are either slaves or subject to slavery at any time." We know that it is only because the people are unarmed and unorganized that the racist pigs are able to ride roughshod over them. Whenever we check out a capitalist situation we find the same thing. Earlier I mentioned Czarist Russia; well, if you check out history you'll find that the Czar and the capitalist regime in Russia was ruled and dominated by a few people. You had the filthy rich on the top along with the nobility and the inner circles of the Czarist regime. You had the peasants who were starving, the masses of the people on the bottom. When you check out Chinese history the same situation applied. In the Congo before Lumumba came to power and then after he was assassinated again you had a few people in control of the economy and wealth of the country and the rest of the people were starving. They used to show pictures of China on a TV program called th[e] Twentieth Century. They showed movies of China before and during its revolutionary war. They used to show the filthy rich and the warlords who plundered the Chinese countryside getting richer and richer while the peasants who were very poor, were getting poorer and poorer. Here again the landlords were pro-western or pro-capitalist and the peasants were pro-communist or pro-eastern. When we check this situation out, we find that in all the countries that have moved to gain their national liberation and 'self-determination' that the people there are moving away from capitalistic stands and towards socialistic or communistic stands. The people in these countries when they begin to fight to control their own destinies realize that as long as the power remains vested in the hands of a few capitalists or in the hands of an exploitative capitalistic class then the people will never gain any people's powers. When we move closer to home and move up to date we can check out the situation in Latin America and we see the same thing occurring that occurred in China and Russia. The all of Latin America is made into a private reserve for the capitalist in America. If you look at Latin America you'll see that before Fidel Castro and the Cuban people took over power in Cuba the power was vested in the hands of Batista. Now, Batista was nothing but a puppet or a tool of U.S. imperialism and U.S. capitalism. At the Hotel Havana Hilton, the rich decadent capitalist pigs of the U.S. used to come to bask in the sun and to carry on "their decadent sexual practices and other perversions." In Bob Dylan's record, "Ballad of the Thin Man" and Mr. Jones, it says that Mr. Jones went to a freak show and paid his money to go in and see the Geak and the Geak was eating raw meat on a bone. Well the Geak gave the bone to Mr. Jones and said "How does it feel to be a freak?" Well, on examination of that we find that what the Geak meant was that he was there eating the raw meat because that was the only way he could survive; but Mr. Jones, who in this case would be the capitalist class in America, was the real freak because he was paying to see someone perform these types of acts. Well, in Cuba, before the power was wrested away from imperialism and its running dogs, all of Havana was one big U.S. playpen. The capitalists in this country created mass prostitution, homosexuality and organized crime with their filthy contamination. When Fidel Castro moved and took the power out of the hands of the capitalist and gave it back to the people we find that U.S. capitalism reacted in a very violent way. Batista was backed to the hilt and excess U.S. 10,000 lb. bombs were sold to Batista and dropped on the Cuban people. Later the U.S. instigated, financed, organized and backed the Bay of Pigs invasion of Cuba that was crushed by the heroic Cuban people's Army. Today, more than a decade later, we find that U.S. capitalism is engaged in another criminal act against the Cuban people which like all the other capitalist plots is bound to fail. The U.S. economic blockade of Cuba. Moving again closer to home we find that here in our black communities if black people want examples of what capitalism is and what its effects are all they have to do is look around in the various prisons and jails. It's not just a coincidence that in all colonies and semi-colonies you have a so-called high crime rate. The rate is directly [related] to the exploitation and oppression by the ruling capitalist class. The crime rate and prostitution rate in our communities is due directly to poor education, poor housing, poor clothing, no jobs, and an ever present hungry stomach. These things again are directly attributed to capitalism and exploitation. The ghettoes in this country are not here by accident. They're a place where a readily available source of cheap manpower can be dumped and stored until it is needed and as a market place for dumping billions of dollars worth of inferior goods and corrupt services. So the ghettoes here in America are not here by accident. They're set up and maintained by capitalists in this country for a specific purpose and design.

Again checking history we find that in the days of slavery there were two classifications. There was the field nigger and there was the house nigger. The field niggers have always outnumbered the house niggers, but the house niggers have worked in conjunction with the slavemaster to help maintain the oppression of their black brothers and sisters. Today we find that these black capitalists that are being set up and fostered by Nixon and the capitalist ruling circles in this country are nothing but the modern day counterparts of the old house niggers, and where the house Negro would get the scraps off of the master's plate, these black capitalists will get the scraps off of these racist white capitalists' plates. To take a particular case in point, we have the example of the Negro who owns the Rainbow Car Wash in East Oakland who says that the only thing that will save the black race is for it to become like the white race and that black people are inferior to white people. We can see just how far a perversion this quest for the scraps from the master's table can become. Also we have the fools who backed Wallace in this last presidential election. In the Bible there is a parable that closely relates to what we are talking about where Christ talked about a crawling Lazarus begging at the gate. This is the same thing as these so-called black capitalists who are begging the white man to let them into the system of exploitation instead of rising up and destroying the very system of exploitation and thereby ridding themselves once and for all of this problem. The slavemaster who in this case is the modern day capitalist is no fool and as long as he could get by without giving up anything he didn't give anything up. Now that black people have increased their cry for justice and freedom and begun to consciously wage guerrilla warfare the capitalist ruling classes in this country who are just world-wide slavemasters, have moved to offer scraps from their table to the people. Checking around we find that Premier Thieu and Vice-President Ky of South Viet Nam are in the positions of house niggers. They are house niggers of Viet Nam. Of the money, prestige and power that rest in their hands little if any of it ever reached down to the people. In China it was the same way. Chiang Kai-shek who was nothing more than a Chinese house nigger, a Chinese capitalist. None of the money and power that was vested in his hands got down to the masses of the Chinese people. All they ever got was the iron boot and the clubs and bullets from Chiang Kai-shek's bandit troops. When we check Cuba the same situation existed. Batista, who was another house nigger, all the people ever got from him ww[a]s surplus 10,000 lb. bombs and U.S. airforce napalm. And in this country black capitalists have the same positions as the Batista's and the Chiang Kai-shek's and the house niggers of American slavery. Of the scraps that are given to them few, if any of them, ever find their way down to the starving masses of people.

So what black people have to realize is that anything that the enemy offers you as a solution to your problem is not correct because your enemy will never give you anything that will aid you in defeating him. What we must do is to make our own definitions and analysis of the situation in order to come up with solutions that will concretely deal with the problem confronting us. In the Black Panther Party we have a plank of our 10-point platform that specifically deals with capitalism. Point No. 3: "We want an end to the robbery by the white man of our black community." When we say this we mean that we want an end to all types of robbery. And end to the robbery of our youth by sending them off 8,000 miles to be murdered and butchered and used as cannon fodder to help sustain a war of imperialist aggression. An end to the robbery and destruction of our children's minds by racist schools and administrations. And end to the robbery and rape of our sisters' bodies by racist capitalist perverts who don't deserve to be called males. An end to the robbery of black men of action by murder and imprisonment on down to the coopting of so-called black leadership by plans such as Nixon's black capitalist plan. The Black Panther Party is a party that is determined to move by any means necessary to obtain good ends. We in the Black Panther Party refuse to be fooled by the word "Black." We realize that capitalism, bureaucratic capitalism as it exists in the world today right now here is our main enemy, and no matter what color prefix you put on it, it still comes out the same. Just as bloody and just as vile as ever. And when we think about capitalism we immediately get frames of reference of napalm and jets in Viet Nam, C.I.A. murders in the Congo and Bolivia, racist pigs.

U.S. paratroopers, and national guard troops running amuck in the black community, and the peoples of the world being murdered. If black people indeed need some outside direction on how to deal with capitalism let us look to the valie[a]nt Vietnamese for the proper types of examples.

27. Nuclear Fraud Betrays World's Peoples' Interest. March 31, 1969. Page 11

To maintain their nuclear hegemony and carry out nuclear blackmail against other countries so as to push their counter-revolutionary "global strategy," U. S. imperialism and Soviet revisionism have for years tried to make a deal over the so-called "nuclear non-proliferation" question. They have become more eager than before to reach an earlier agreement on this question since China

successfully conducted a number of nuclear tests which have struck terror into their hearts. They cooked up a so-called "treaty on non-proliferation of nuclear weapons" at the beginning of 1968 after compromises and concessions were made by the Soviet revisionists, and manipulated the U. N. General Assembly into adopting it last June. Under this treaty, not only can the U. S. imperialists and the Soviet revisionists produce and stockpile nuclear weapons and expand their nuclear bases, they make no commitments whatsoever not to use nuclear weapons against the non-nuclear states. The non-nuclear states, however, are totally deprived of their right to develop nuclear weapons for self-defense and are even restricted in the use of atomic energy for peaceful purposes. To put it bluntly, the treaty is something imposed on the non-nuclear states to bind them hand and foot. The Soviet revisionists also joined with the U. S. imperialists in manipulating the U. N. Security Council into adopting a so-called "nuclear protection" plan, scheming to turn the non-nuclear states into their "protectorates" so as to control and subjugate them at will. Scared out of their wits by the remarkable progress of socialist China in the development of guided missiles and nuclear weapons, Soviet revisionism and U. S. imperialism have in the past few years intensified their collusion against China on the nuclear question. In fact, the Soviet revisionists have formed a nuclear military alliance with the U. S. imperialists against China. At present, further deals are in the brew between Soviet revisionism and U. S. imperialism on the so-called question of "limiting the anti-ballistic missile race." Not long ago, the Soviet revisionists deliberately chose the day of Nixon's inauguration to issue a "statement of the Soviet Union on the policy of the disarmament question," brazenly praising the counter-revolutionary deals between the Soviet Union and the Unites States on the question of nuclear weapons and expressing the hope of the Soviet revisionists to reach further agreement with U. S. imperialism on the "curbing of the strategic arms race." The U. S. imperialist boss Nixon openly expressed his appreciation of this. Many heinous moves of the Soviet revisionist renegade clique made in collusion with U. S. imperialism under the cloak of "nuclear disarmament" constitute an additional grave crime in betraying the interests of the people the world over and in allying with U. S. imperialism to oppose China.

28. Inducing & Forcing Arab People To Surrender. March 31, 1969. Page 15

To push the social-imperialist policy of expansion in the Middle East, stamp out the raging flames of the people's revolutionary struggle there and enslave the Arab people, the Soviet revisionist renegade clique has long been colluding and at the same time contending with U. S. Imperialism in this area. It takes counter-revolutionary "joint actions" with the U. S. Imperialists to suppress the Arab people, acting as the biggest accomplice of U. S. Imperialism.

The large-scale U.S.-Israeli war of aggression against the Arab countries in 1967 was launched with the tacit consent and connivance of the Soviet revisionists. Brazenly playing the Counterrevolutionary dual tactics, the Soviet renegades while verbally rendering support to the Arab people's "actions against aggression" actually collaborated closely with U. S, Imperialism. They worked zealously hand in glove with the U.S. Imperialists--from diplomatic activities to political collaboration, from behind-the-scenes "dealings" to open "alliance" from the exchanges of secret envoys to the dialogue through the "hot line", etc. Together with U. S. Imperialism they manipulated the United Nations into forcing the Arab countries to "cease fire" under the situation that large areas of the Arab territory were occupied by Israel. The Soviet revisionist chieftain Kosygin even went to Glassboro personally o give advice to the them U. S. Imperialist boss Johnson and to devise secretly with him sinister plots for suppressing the revolutionary struggle of the Arab people.

Since a secret agreement was reached in Glassboro, U.S. Imperialism and Soviet revisionism have stepped up, in a big fanfare, their efforts to cook up a big fraud on the "political settlement" of the Middle East question. Under the manipulation, the U.C. Security Council adopted a "resolution" on "solving" the Middle East question which was followed by a "seven -point program" put forward by U. S. Imperialism and a "five-point plan" by Soviet Revisionism. Although these "plan" and program" are different in forms, they are common in their counterrevolutionary character. All of them are aimed at peddling the "political settlement" fraud in a vain attempt to completely strangle the cause for liberation of Palestine; to stamp out the armed struggle of the Palestine people, to force the Arab countries to capitulate to the U.S.-Israeli aggressors, to establish joint U.S.-Soviet domination over the Middle East and to enslave the Arab people.

Around the time of Nixon's inauguration, the Soviet Revisionists were carrying out more energetically their sinister activities on the Middle East question. Meanwhile, the Nixon administration which has landed itself in an impasse is trying to "calm down" the "explosive" Middle East situation by striking a "package deal" on all-round collusion with the Soviet Revisionists. A "four power conference" for suppressing the Arab people's struggle is now being vigorously planned by the United States and the Soviet Union. As revealed by Nixon at a press conference several days ago, the Soviet Revisionists have already made a dirty deal with U.S. Imperialism on the Middle East question behind the back of the Arab people.

(This article is reprinted from the *Tricontinental*, organ of OSPAAL - The Organization of the Solidarity of the Peoples of Africa, Asia and Latin America.)

YAKARTA, Indonesia (INS) - Even though the news from Indonesia does not always get front page coverage in the newspapers, the situation that the Indonesian people, oppressed by a fascist tyranny, continue to face, is alarmingly dramatic.

The anti-Communist regime headed by General Suharto has continued its policy of mass physical sectors of the country.

The number of persons -accused of membership in or collaboration with the Communist Party-who have been assassinated has reached more than a million.

Suharto, together with the reactionary general Nasution, assumed the real power in Indonesia at the end of September, 1965, reducing the then President Sukarno to a nominal role. Suharto has, since then, put into practice a policy of open submission to U.S. imperialism.

In March, 1966, the militarist maneuver against Sukarno was consummated, and he was removed from the positions he had held. Suharto, who became President through reactionary means, stepped up the mass murders, the abuses and the jailings, opened the ports to foreign monopolies and returned to the landowners and national capitalists the property that had been nationalized.

In Indonesia, imperialism, has reversed the objectives of the nationalist government of Sukarno, converting the nation into a beachhead against the people of Southeast Asia.

In payment for this, the Suharto regime has received $312 million in "aid" this year, supplied by several capitalist governments, among them, of course, the United States and West Germany.

In spite of this "aid," all the regime's development plans have failed as a result of the embezzlement and misuse of public funds that has brought economic chaos to Indonesia. The news agency, Antara, recently reported that the number of unemployed workers in Indonesia, by the end of the month of August, had reached 8,700,000 and pointed out that in July alone 12,000 workers had been fired from state enterprises.

According to Antara, one of the causes of increasing unemployment, is that the Indonesian market has been flooded with foreign products (which the people cannot buy). About 80 percent of the textile mills have closed down or cut back production, leaving 500,000 workers unemployed. Regarding the situation in the countryside, where 80 percent of the population lives, it is noteworthy that a great number of peasants are constantly moving to the large cities in a vain attempt to find work to mitigate their hunger. The flow to Jakarta is so great that the agency describes it as "the world capital of vagabonds."

But while all this is happening, the vanguard in Indonesia is not remaining idle. Guerilla movements organized by the

Communist Party, (other progressive movements have been invited to join) and are operating in several areas of the country, including East Java, Sumatra, Sulawesi, Ambon Ball, and West and Central Kalimantan.

For the 105 million inhabitants of the Pacific Islands that make up the Indonesian archipelago, this is a time of suffering and hardship, but it is also a time of sustained anti-imperialist struggle which has the sympathy and support of the progressive forces of the world.

30. SERVING THE PEOPLE APRIL 6, 1969. PAGE 14.

The Black Panther Party is a political party established to create revolutionary political power for Black People and is continuing steadily to serve the People heart and soul. . . Our Cardinal Rule is: "Have faith in the People, and faith in the Party." This faith derives from an undying love for our people and the awareness of a need for governmental eclipse. We, as the vanguard of the oppressed masses, realize that we must and will serve the People heart and soul. The need and wants of the People must be fulfilled, and we, as Huey P. Newton says, shall be like an oxen to be ridden by the People. The exploited and oppressed people's needs are land, bread, housing, education, freedom, clothing, justice and peace and the Black Panther Party shall not, for a single day, alienate ourselves from the masses and forget their needs for survival, but instead institute to the People faith to the death.

"I'd rather be without the shame, A bullet lodged within my brain. If I were not to reach our goal Let bleeding cancer torment my soul." - Bunchy.

It is only the People that can overthrow the present imperialistic environment that we are exposed to and only the People can institute a socialistic government that will serve them. The spirit of the People is greater than the man's technology, and that spirit will be guided by the vanguard party of this present liberation struggle. The capitalistic, imperialistic, doggish, pimping of the People must cease by this wanton, sadistic country or perish like Babylon. The People shall smash the glutton roaches running this decadent society and, along with the directing of the Black Panther Party, halt these running dogs and gain true liberation for all. We cannot depend upon the present government to fulfill our wants and needs. Thus more and more programs shall be set up to suffice the desires of the People and destroy the dictatorship of the bourgeoisie (ruling class) and its lackeys. The Black Panther Party is for everything that the enemy (U. S. imperialists) is against, and against everything the enemy is for. We believe in serving the People whole-heartedly in a socialistic manner, not spending money like the U. S. to take hung er surveys, but to feed the People. All our actions are to the exact opposite of this hypocrisy called democracy. The Black Panther Party will continue to serve the people and fulfill their every desire as an International united front of revolutionarie s of the world, battling this mass oppression of capitalism and imperialism. When people call in to say they need food, we do not spout a lot of superficial rhetoric, but see that they are fed. "Our duty is to hold ourselves responsible to the People. Every word, every act, and every policy must conform to the People's interest and, if mistakes occur, they must be corrected - that is what being responsible to the People means. - Mao Tse-Tung - Marsha

31. Imperialism, White Chauvinism And Pl.
April 20, 1969. Page 7.

The farcical trial in Memphis, Tennessee, proved that 1) any Black man, regardless of class or fame, can be murdered by agents of the ruling 60 families, and 2) that there was a conspiracy to murder Reverend (Martin Luther) King. Immediately prior to Reverend King's murder, President Johnson publicly supported the white-supremacist, Klan-ridden Memphis police force. Large numbers of F.B.I. men were working with the Memphis police; Reverend King was surrounded by Memphis police and F.B.I. men when shot. James Reston, the *New York Times* Washington editor, played a leading role in hunting up Johnson's and J. Edgar Hoover's role in the murder of Reverend King. Now the *New York Times* "regrets" the farcical court actions in Memphis while still covering up the role of Johnson and Hoover. The *Times* wants those who urged attacks on Reverend King to determine if there was a conspiracy. This is the "free" press in action. In our newsletter of May, 1968, we reported the lynching of a Black man in South Boston. Three white men were arrested. The "prosecution" first reduced the charge to second-degree murder. Then an all-white jury could not agree - mistrial. The next step will be, if the usual system of white supremacy prevails, either a suspended sentence or complete freedom for the lynchers.

With the above events in mind, consider Progressive Labor's attack on Eldridge Cleaver, Black Panther leader. The PL magazine, page 33 of the February, 1969 edition, says, "Some of the reasons he (Cleaver) gave for not returning to jail were that prison would be too rough for him, because he is an intellectual or because he can't take it any more. We state that every Black man has the right and duty to stay out of imperialist jails. This, like all other questions, is a political question. But to see jail only in personal terms without any relationship to the entire movement and to run to save one's own skin, is giving no political leadership." PL, with Mao's support, has done everything possible to slander, expose and jail every Black nationalist leader. PL used the prestige of Chinese support and urged Malcolm X to work openly. PL attacked Reverend King's support to Black garbage workers in Memphis, thus covering up the conspirators against Reverend King. Note that PL claims it opposes the jailing of Black men in general. But Black leaders should surrender! If PL leaders feel it is so wrong for a Black leader such as Robert Williams or Cleaver to avoid jail, "to run away," then what is their practice? To keep them from running away, to help the F. B. I. find them, is the only conclusion that can be drawn from PL's position. [MIM comments: This is the only negative reference to Mao we found in the Black Panther Party literature, and we believe it is appropriate, because Mao did originally recognize PL (Progressive Labor) as a fraternal communist party. PL split from Mao in 1969 and thereafter pioneered crypto-Trotskyism and integrationism on imperialist terms.]

32. Excerpt Of An Interview With The Chief Of Staff David Hilliard. April 20, 1969. Page 18

You speak of the strength and organization of the Longshore-men but do you think they will be able to fight off the ill effects of containerization without the help of the community? A.: I doubt it. They will not need the community to retain their right to work, in terms of loading and unloading the vans. I think that it will probably be solved in the next two weeks. We have seen in the past that they have come up with threats of walking out or striking, but we know that the waterfronts are a major means of export and importation here in North America. I don't think they (employers) could stand the economic effect of having the longshoremen go out. Because they need the longshoremen for more reasons than containers.

So they will give them another one of the concessions out of the bag?

That's right. So, they will gladly concede to those demands in order to further their imperialistic means. To further ex-ploitation and prolong their war on the Vietnamese people. The longshoremen play an important part in that because they work at the military bases.

What is the reason for the purge that is going on in the Black Panther Party?

We related to what Lenin said, "that a party that purges itself grows to become stronger." The purging is very good. You recognize that there is a diffusion within the rank and file of the party, within the internal structure of the party. So the very fact that you purge strengthens the party. You get rid of all the criminal elements, and work with the people left. You will become stronger, more of a fortress. Quoting form Stalin, I think he said something like "the party used to be hospitable, it would yield to the opinions of all the sympathizers. "But, now the party has become like a fortress." And that the party is only interested in the very best and the most revolutionary sections of society. We try now to attract the very best. And our doors are not open to anyone that decides that they want to join the party. Now the people that become a part of the rank and file of the Black Panther Party will definitely have to be somebody who wants to carry out the desires and aspirations of the oppressed people."

What of the alliance with DRUM FRUM?

That was an alliance that was put together by Kenny Horston. He is the leader of the Black Panther Caucus out at General Motors in Fremont. Kenny had went back east to do some investigation because he became interested in trying to organize the workers, the black workers in particular. He went back and had discussions with members of DRUM and members of the Ford revolutionary movement that they have back there. He found out that the majority of the members within the two organizations were Panther Party members. That was a very gladdening experience to know, that the brothers back there hand begun to organize the workers. And really moving to try and put up a working class force in order to deliver a very mighty and telling blow to the imperialistic system. I think the credit should be attributed to Kenny Horston the brother that came up with the idea of trying to make some coalition with the Black Caucus here in Fremont, and the brothers in Detroit. We see the necessity of making some alliances with the working class, black, white, Latin American, Orientals, and or what have you. We see that as being a very grave necessity that the revolution as a whole is dependent upon making a coalition with the other working class people. Panthers themselves are workers, it is just that we consider ourselves the most advanced detachment of the working class. Because of the theoretical analysis and because we have applied theoretically the ideas and works of Marx and Lenin and we have tested them in the external world, which proves that there is a need for the masses of the people, and a need for solidarity of the working class. Our whole thing about discovering the triumvirate consisting of Lenin, Trotsky and Stalin. It is just a matter of trying to give a very complete picture of history. It's like considering the part without the whole to talk about Lenin and Marx, to talk about Mao Tse Tung and his deed without really bringing Stalin in on the overall historical scene. Stalin played a very important part in the Russian revolution and he played an important part in the first Socialist State manifested in Russia. It is not a thing that we are Maoist or Stalinist, Leninist. We say that there is no such animal as a Maoist --- that there is just Marxist, Leninist, and that Stalin was truly a Marxist-Leninist. He always praised Lenin and carried out the ideas of Lenin. It's just a matter of people and history in its totality and telling the true story of what took place. The reason that they fear Joseph Stalin is because of the distorted facts that they have gained through the Western press. The one thing that we respect about Stalin, is that Stalin was able to capture the will of the people. He was able to put forth the will of the people more so than anyone else.

[MC5 comments: At that time Mao himself denied there was Maoism. He called himself "Marxist-Leninist." Since that time, we of MIM and a few others in the world have started to speak of "Maoism" to enshrine the contributions Mao made in fighting the bourgeoisie under socialism. The phrase "Marxism-Leninism-Maoism" or just "Maoism" indicates that Mao raised Marxism-Leninism to a third stage of development.]

33. Why We Support China.
April 20, 1969. Page 20

It seems highly unlikely that the intentional involvement of the United States Airforce plans, in the intrusion into and the exercising of territorial domain over parts of Laos called the Ho Chi Minh trail, is a random move. This involvement is designed to coincide with the United States undercover Pig the Soviet Union of Russia. Trends in this country to form closer ties to the Soviet Union and the experts of the Soviet Union to reciprocate are further indications of the revisionism, which has led the people of Russia and the people under her control, i.e. Hungary, Poland, Czechoslovokia, Romania, East Germany and Yugoslavia closer into the gaping jaws of colonialism and the searing teeth of capitalism and has produced the aggressive movements of Russian troops and cut out movements of Russian troops and diplomatic barks thrown at our brothers in China. This move then must be taken as an endorsement of the war in Viet Nam, otherwise how could it be possible for the campaigns to proceed simultaneously. Is it so diametrically unopposed to one another over night. Or could the avaricious fools who dictate foreign policy have for both countries decided that even though they differ somewhat when they are dealing with a "Civilized Country," means anything that has a white or a white thinking puppet when it comes to dealing with a non-oppressive or non-white country, their differences cease to exist. Marxist-Leninist theory indicates that we must unite with real friends in order to distinguish real enemies, and we all know that capitalism is our real enemy. Marxist-Leninist practice because it is nice to never become divorced from practice, proves out the theory that anything that our enemy attacks must not be all bad for us, and anything that our enemy does not attack cannot be all good for us and in most cases will be more good than bad. We know capitalism is our enemy. Capitalism is the United States government and the U.S. government is capitalism. The U.S. is preparing for directly and is attacking indirectly the People's Republic of China; it is not yet attacking the Soviet Union. Unite with real friends in order to defeat real enemies. There is too much co-existing with the oppressor. There is one common denominator that is very glaring in the previous sentence in each case there are two dominant classes, the haves and the have nots, the oppressor and the oppressed. China stands as a beacon to all revolutionaries around the world: the guiding light showing the path to freedom to all of our brothers in Africa and Asia. For this and only this reason has she been singled out for attack. The imperialists in Russia and the U.S. realize in their cunning that if they can stop the revolutionary and dynamic thrust, of China, them and their lackeys, with no China to face can continue to subjugate and exploit Africa, Asia, Latin America, Harlem, Watts, Oakland and your neighborhood wherever you may happen to be, but what they don't realize is that you and I will not let them. FREE HUEY PANTHER POWER TO THE VANGUARD BLACK POWER TO BLACK PEOPLE - FREE HUEY

Raymond Jennings, East Oakland branch, BPP

34. Statement By The Central Committee of The Black Panther Party. April 27, 1969. Page 14.

Twenty one New York Black Panther Party members busted by pig power structure. Statement from the Black Panther Party Central Committee at National Headquarters, Oakland, California, delivered by the Deputy Chairman, David Brothers of the New York State Black Panther Party Central Staff. Historically, all reactionary forces (the pig power structure and their "cultural" Black capitalist lackeys) on the verge of Extinction invariably conduct a last desperate struggle against the revolutionary forces (all workers, the unemployed, Mexicans, Indians, Puerto Ricans, poor whites, et. al., but especially poor black and oppressed peoples and their vanguard, the Black Panther Party. And some revolutionaries are apt to be deluded for a time by this phenomenon of outward strength but inner weakness, failing to grasp the essential fact that the enemy is nearing extinction while they themselves (the revolutionary peoples) are nearing victory. (Mao's little *Red Book*, page 83) Two million one hundred thousand dollars bail and the charges against the 21 Black Panther Party members is absurd and outrageous.

Concerning the charges, every Black Panther Party chapter and leadership knows that we would not waste dynamite on the blowing up of some jive railway stations and department stores simply because some of our own poor people would be killed and we know this is completely wrong when it comes to organizing the people against the demogogue politicians, the avaricious businessmen, and the racist pig police forces. They are the enemies of the people of America, be they white, brown, black, yellow or red. We will not try to fight fire with fire because all of the people that fire is best put out with water. Therefore, the Black Panther Party will not fight racism with racism. But we will fight racism with solidarity. We will not fight capitalism with capitalism (Black capitalism), but with the implementation of socialism and socialist programs for the people. We will not fight U.S. government imperialism with more imperialism because the peoples of the world and other races, especially in America, must fight imperialism with proletarian internationalism. All peoples and revolutionaries must defend themselves with organized guns and force when attacked by the pig power structure.

"The socialist system will eventually replace the capitalist-racist system; this is an objective law independent of man's will. However much the reactionaries try to hold back the wheel of history, sooner or later revolution will take place and will inevitably triumph." (Mao's little Red Book, page 24) The Black Panther Party is informing and calling on all the peoples of the communities across the country to scorn and denounce the actions of this capitalist-racist government's attempts to try and destroy the Black Panther Party which has chapters and branches across the nation. Scorn, denounce, and destroy the lies by capitalists and racists, from the nixons, the rockefellers, and all their pig lackeys, to the bootlicking cultural nationalists and black capitalists. They are the real conspirators where we see their obvious attempts to destroy the black panther party's revolutionary leadership. They, of course, try to do this by murders, jailings, unfair court trials, the forcing of eldridge cleaver into exile, and the temporary imprisonment of the minister of defense, Huey P. Newton in california. Free Huey. The revolution is here. We the people of the world must free Huey and all political prisoners because if it wasn't for Huey P. Newton, free breakfast for children programs before school would not be spreading across the nation. If it wasn't for Huey P. Newton, the idea of having free medicine and free health clinics wouldn't be in the process of being implemented. If it wasn't for huey p. Newton, the teaching that "it's not a race struggle, but a class struggle" would not begin to be understood.

IF IT WASN'T FOR HUEY P. NEWTON, THE TEN POINT PLATFORM AND PROGRAM OF THE BLACK PANTHER PARTY WOULD NOT BE IN THE PROCESS OF BEING IMPLEMENTED, PRACTICAL SOCIALIST PROGRAMS FROM THE BLACK NATION IS WHERE IT'S AT, WHEN EVEN OTHER ETHNIC GROUPS COPY IT, AND THE PEOPLES OF THE WORLD KNOW THIS IS THEIR AND THAT IT'S RIGHT. THE NEW YORK BLACK PANTHER PARTY 21 MUST BE SET FREE AS HUEY P. NEWTON MUST BE SET FREE. THEY, AND ALL OTHER POLITICAL PRISONERS, MUST RECEIVE THE PEOPLE'S SUPPORT AS A NATIONAL RESISTANCE AGAINST THE PIG POWER STRUCTURE WHICH IS IMPERIALISTIC, CAPITALISTIC AND RACIST. A NATION-WIDE CAMPAIGN IS NOW IN THE PROCESS OF BEING WAGED TO PUT TOGETHER A "FREE POLITICAL

PRISONERS FOR THE PEOPLE'S REVOLUTIONARY STRUGGLE." THE NEW YORK BLACK PANTHER PARTY 21 MUST BE SET FREE. BAIL MONEY IS NEEDED FOR THE 21, HUEY P. NEWTON, EL- DRIDGE CLEAVER, AND "THE CONSPIRACY 8" OF CHICAGO, WITH BOBBY SEALE, BLACK PANTHER PARTY CHAIRMAN. DO- NATIONS MAY BE SENT TO: LEGAL DEFENSE FUND BLACK PAN- THER PARTY BOX 1224 POWER TO ALL THE PEOPLE PANTHER POWER TO THE VANGUARD

35. Revolutionary Heros. May 11, 1969. Page 4.

Jose Rios Mario Martinez Nelson Rodrigues "One Pig Dead -- One Wounded Brown Brothers Beat The Heat" Pigs in San Francisco have stepped up their repression of the Black and Brown community. They are committing murder at will; they are busting in doors and ripping of the people's property. Mayor Pig Alioto has chosen a top flight crew of murderous pigs to patrol and control the Brown and Black Communities of San Francisco. On May 1st, May Day, the day of the gigantic Free Huey rally, two of Alioto's top executioners vamped on the brothers from the Brown Community who were attending to their own affairs. These brothers, who are endowed with the revolutionary spirit of the Black Panther Party defended themselves from the racist pig gestapo. Pig Joseph Brodnik received his just reward with a big hole in the chest. Pig Paul McGoran got his in the mouth which was not quite enough to off him. The revolutionary brothers escaped the huge swarm of pigs with dogs, mace, tanks and helicopters, proving once again that "the spirit of the people is greater than the man's technology." To these brothers the revolutionary people of racist America want to say, by your revolutionary deed you are heroes, and that you are always welcome to our camp.

36. Black Panther Revolutionary Wedding. May 11, 1969. Page 7

On May Day, Thursday, May 1st a revolutionary wedding took place. The wedding was to unite in revolutionary matrimony, Black Panther Brother Charles Bursey and Panther Sister Shelly Sanders. The wedding was the first of its kind here in the decadent, racist America. The ceremony was performed at the Church of the Minister of Religion of the Black Panther Party, Father Earl Neil. The Church is located at 27th and West Streets in West Oakland. The Church is also the site of one of the Black Panther Party's Free Breakfast for Children programs. The ceremony was officially carried out by the National Chairman of the Black Panther Party, Bobby Seale. In place of a Holy Bible, Chairman Bobby used the Red Book "Quotations from Chairman Mao Tse-tung." The crowd attending the wedding consisted mostly of Panther members and children from the community, who attended the breakfast program every morning. The marrying couple looked radiantly revolutionary in their Panther uniforms of black and Panther blue. After the ceremony, the united couple were serenaded by the children to the revolutionary song of "We want a pork chop, off the pig."

37. Republic Of New Africa Denounces Ron Everett (Karenga). May 11, 1969 Page 7

From: The Minister of State and Foreign Affairs of the Republic of New Africa. TO: Brother Bobby Seale In the Name of Peace and Power to the People: Dear Brother Seale, There was convened in the City of Detroit on April 5, 1969, a meeting of the legislative assembly of the Republic of New Africa. At this meeting, it was officially reported that Ron Karenga was directed to explain the accusation and his responsibility, if any, in the action that ended in the death of two Panther Brothers on the campus at U.C.L.A.

38. Chairman Bobby Speaks At May Day Rally To Free Huey. May 11, 1969. Page 11

What's happening people? (Free Huey) Good evening, Good morning. I think it's about 12:00 right now. It's about 12:00 and if you look in the back of you, you will see Reagan's state building, with his state pigs observing the people. And, of course, if you look in front of you, you will see Nixon's U.S. federal building, with the pigs inside, observing the people. and if later on you decide to leave here and go on down Polk Street, you'll walk in front of pig mayor Alioto's office, and they'll be observing the people. Now I know you've heard a lot lately about what pig Mafioso, Moussili, Alioto, has had to say, (right on I know you've heard this pig with his ignorant backwards, minded butt sit up and say crazy things, like he wants to destroy the Black Panther Party. But the Black Panther Party, and black people, and Mexican-American people, and all people are saying there will always be Huey P. Newton, and a Black Panther Party, as long as there are black people living here in this city. (right on). Pig mayor Alioto said that he wanted to destroy the Black Panther Party. Richard Nixon, from the United States White House, is saying that he wants to destroy the Black Panther Party, by lying

143

to the people, (right on) and by not telling the truth; and the reason they're not telling the truth is 'cause they always told lies. Right on. They told lies about the people, trying to protect their own self-capitalist interests. In the papers this morning (and I want the papers to get ahold of this) they're saying or trying to imply that the Black Panther Party is "subversive." Well, this is all the Black Panther Party has to say to all those pigs in the power structure. The Black Panther Party, along with other members of the community are feeding 2,000 young brothers and sisters every morning (right on), if that's subversive, then damn it we're subversive. (More right on's). The Black Panther Party is going forth implement Free Health Clinics in the black community, and we hope the Mexican-Americans, and the Chinese-Americans and all the other people do the same thing -- and if Free Health Clinics are subversive then damnit, mayor Alioto, and pig Reagan and Nixon, damnit, we're subversive. (Right on). We're saying that the Ten Point Platform and Program that our Minister of Defense Huey P. Newton put together, is in the process of being implemented. That if it had not been for Huey P. Newton we would not have people with an understanding that they got a right to use weapons to defend themselves against any pigs who attack them. (Right on.) We're saying that if it had not been for Huey P. Newton, there would not be any Breakfast For Children. (Right on.) If it had not been for Huey P. Newton Community Control Of Police would not be in the process of being implemented by the people. If it had not been for Huey P. Newton, Free Health Clinics would not be in the process of being implemented in the black community. If it had not been for Huey P. Newton, the Ten Point Platform And Program of the Black Panther Party would not begin to be implemented by the people. And not only black people, because the Chinese-American, the Red Guard, has copied the same Platform and Program, and they got a right to it. And the Indian-American organization named NARP has copied the same Ten Point Platform and Program of the Black Panther Party and they got a right to it. We're just waiting for this racism to break down when we see in the poor white Appalachians up in the mountains copy the same Ten Point Platform and Program and go forth to destroy the Nixons, the Reagans, and the pig Aliotos. (Right on.) When the Party says "Power to the People, " we ain't jiving a pound. We say Power To The People. And when the people say to Reagan, when the people say to Alioto, when the people say to pig Richard M. Nixon, that we want Huey P. Newton free, we're saying you bald headed pig punks better get out of the way (Right on.) because we're tired. And we saying you better let Huey go. They let that pig O'Brien, who killed Basket go, right on. You let him go on the very minute you allowed him in the street to murder our brothers. They let that other pig go who killed Brother Lindstrom out in Hunter's Point (right on). Wait a minute, the Young Men of [no text --ed.] And this damn bald-headed Mafioso, Alioto jumped up talking about (right on), wait a minute, the Young Men of Action are his boys. Aint he an ass-hole, shame. (Right on.) What we're saying is this. We're saying this here. We heard the brothers say in a press conference the brothers in Young Men of Action, they said in a press conference that they denounced pig mayor Alioto, and mayor Alioto is saying that that's his boys. But we're saying this here: the Panther Party aint mayor Alioto's boys. (laughter) We are the people's workers, and we're going to keep serving the people, everybody. I mean everybody. The man don't like it, but we gone show him. You got your Red Books, hold your Red Books up and tell the brothers where we getting some new ideology from. We're saying like Huey P. Newton said, "that we're going to follow the thoughts of Chairman Mao." We're saying we going . . . Panther Party standing up and proving through social practice that we're not racist, but proving that they in fact are the real racists. They have never liked the Black Panther Party and the people talk about "We want some community control of police." They have never respected Huey P. Newton. But we respect Huey

P. Newton. We love Huey P. Newton. (Right on.) I say: We love Huey P. Newton (repeated). We love Eldridge Cleaver (repeated). We love Kathleen Cleaver. We love all our people. We love our people so much that if the pigs attack us, we gone defend ourselves rightfully with guns and force. (Right on.) We love the people (audience repeats) and we love the people so much that we gone say: I am a revolutionary and that's our message to pig Alioto and Richard M. Nixon's America. That you and Free Huey, (repeated). Free Huey. Free Huey. Some Brothers are walking around with some buckets, some plastic buckets, they gone be asking for some donations for all the money that had to be put out, and we had to borrow it, to put this rally over, and so let's get it together, there some more speakers coming, sister Kathleen Cleaver is here, Eldridge Cleaver's wife, the Chief of Staff David Hilliard is here, we gone donate to the bucket, because are what, we say: I am a revolutionary. (Audience repeats each statement): Free Huey

P. Newton. Down with the pigs. Down with all the pigs. Power to all the people. The collection is going on. Power to the people and thank you brothers and sisters. Right on. Applause.

39. Persecution Of The Young Lords. May 19, 1969. Page 14

In this country where illegality is systematic and injustice deliberate, not only Black people but Brown people as well, suffer the brunt of repression. The American eagle, with its predatory instincts, vamps and Miss Liberty, with her deliberate ruthlessness, tramples on those people they find it profitable to attack and crush. America compresses its oppressed between an atmosphere of vileness and a ground of hostile instability and dares them to challenge the mediums. The Young Lords Organization, a Latin-American revolutionary group who are working in Chicago, have dared to dispel the mediums; they are demanding an end to the injustices heaved upon Latin-American people. Latin-American people in this country face some of the same problems that we, Black people face, i.e., inadequate food, indecent housing, irrelevant education, police brutality, and unemployment. And what are the Young Lords doing? They are working for adequate food, decent housing, relevant education, police brutality cessation, and employment for their people. The power structure would have these problems continue, as people who have little power to solve these problems are easy to exploit. The Young Lords, however, cannot be placed into this category because they are showing their people the strategic method to resist the oppressive forces of the power structure. This has made them the "enemy" to the power structure and the "friend" to all who desire an end to imperialism. The power structure's perception of them has resulted in them being harassed, arrested, beaten, and shot by the pigs who "protect and serve" (yes, protect capitalistic enterprises and serve us with arrest warrants, search warrants, subpoenas, summons, and the like). On Sunday, April 4, one of the Young Lords, Manuel Ramos, Minister of Defense was killed and Ralph Rivera, Minister of Education was critically wounded. yes these two were dedicating their lives to the revolutionary struggle. They were shot by pigs who made it their goal to deal with them as all protesting poor and exploited people are dealt with: elimination. These brothers who sought to overtake those who have unjustly taken over, whose love was liberation and hate was oppression, whose bodies lie stiff and contorted, whose blood overflows the State of Illinois and surges into those adjacent states, who words (Todo eo poder a la genta -- All power to the people) can be heard reverberating in response to the scream of the oppressed - these brothers we hold sacred; these brothers we hold dearest; these brothers we hold highest. Presently facing many trumped up charges (such as mob action, disorderly conduct, inciting to riot, and everything else that is false) Chairman of the Young Lords, Cha Cha Jimenez is picked up at least once a week by the pigs. Many other Young Lords as well have been arrested on similar conspired charges. The news media and the pigs would have us believe that the Young Lords are a menacing gang, but we know otherwise. Their continuous community efforts have proven this. But the massive intimidations and negative propaganda have not made the Young Lords cease their struggle for the liberation of their people -- quite the contrary. More determined than ever, they are now intensifying their efforts to see that the needs of their people are met. We ask the people to witness the Young Lords as they attempt to improve their community and place its control in the hands of the Latin-American people, to witness the pig persecution of those who believe that power should be vested in the people and not in minority enterprises. We call on the people to judge whether the struggle for justice now being waged by the Young Lords is invalid; whether the murder of one and the intended murder of the other is right. We call on the people to judge whether the Young Lords deserve such persection. Regarding you, the Young Lords, as our true revolutionary brothers, as our comrades, and as our allies, the Black Panther Party is working jointly with you to see that aggression is thwarted and suppression is ended. Illinois Chapter Reporter Carletta Fields

40. Young Lord Murdered By Off Duty Pig. May 19, 1969. Page 14

On May 4, 1969 an off-duty pig who works twenty-four hours a day murdering oppressed people, took the life of one revolutionary brother (Manuel Ramos) and left another lying there seriously wounded. Both of these brothers were shot in the head. Both Brothers were members of the Central Staff of the revolutionary party. These brothers and the Young Lord organization have continued to "practice" revolutionary ideology. They pattern themselves after the Black Panther Party; they identify with the class struggle and that makes us class brothers. When the news was out about this premeditated murder, the community was up in arms, but it was Cha Cha (Chairman) and the Lords that said let's educate, let's organize and let's arm ourselves. Let's inform the community of the pigs' attempt to wipe out the Young Lords. The Young Lords will be opening a free Breakfast program to meet the needs of the people. Power to the People Panther Power to the Black Panther Party Young Lord Power to the Young Lords.

41. Open Letter To Ronald Reagan. May 31, 1969 Page 14

Panther Andrew Austin teaches national guardsmen about Red Book.

Ronald Reagan you're a fool, the people says you're a fool. You've got three to five thousand little fools running around Berkeley with guns even calling you a fool. Now how are you going to deal with that? There were many people who didn't believe me (and you still don't) when I said I held a Redbook class with your National Guards. They told me seeing was believing. Now they believe, what about you Reagan? Your own little punks are being haunted for knowledge from Chairman Mao Tse Tung's Redbook. You see Reagan the Black Panther Party will not allow you to bluff us and hinder us from teaching the masses of people the correct principles and ideologies of revolution. Even after receiving your arrogant and narrow minded orders not to accept reading material from the people, well your troops still read our Black Panther Party Newspapers, and other materials.

When you own little puppets call on the Black Panther Party to teach them passages from Chairman Mao Tse Tung's Redbook such as Imperialism will not last long, because it always does evil things. It persists in grooming and supporting reactionaries in all countries who are against the people, it has forcibly seized many colonies and semi-colonies and many military bases, and it threatens the peace with Atomic war. Thus, forced by Imperialism to do so, more than 90 percent of the world is rising up in struggle against it. Yet, Imperialism is still alive, still running amuck in Asia, Africa and Latin America. In the West Imperialism is still oppressing the people at home. This situation must change. It is the task of the people of the world to put an end to the aggression and oppression perpetuated by imperialism, and chiefly by the U.S. Imperialism. And if the U. S. monopoly capitalist groups persist in pushing their policies of aggression and war, the day is bound to come when they will be hanged by the people of the world. The same fate awaits the accomplices of the United States. So Reagan my last statement is a warning, our Minister of Defense Huey P. Newton says "the spirit of the people is greater than man's technology". And the Black Panther Party is going to continue to educate Black people in the black community, the Mexican Americans, Indian American, Chinese and the oppressor country radical, and even your own little fools running around the streets in Berkeley with guns, to Chairman Mao's Redbook, the Party platform and program, and the People's Revolution. All Power To The People.

A field nigger.

42. Universities Belong To The People.
June 14, 1969 Page 17

Peking, May 24 (Hsinhua) - The struggle of students in some Latin American countries against fascist suppression by the reactionary authorities and against the decadent educational system is continuing to surge forward. It has won the warm support of the working class. The recent killing of a number of students by the reactionary pro U.S. government in Argentina has evoked great indignation among the students and labouring people of the country. In defiance of suppression by the reactionary authorities, University and middle school students in the capital Buenos Aires and many other cities continued to hold demonstrations on May 22. In La Plata City, the demonstrating students shouted: 'Ongania, assain!' They distributed leaflets and erected street barricades to resist police suppression. In Cordoba City, students of two private schools announced the occupation of the school buildings. In Mendoza City, 2,000 University students held a demonstration to demand the resignation of the Minister of the Interior for his direct responsibility in the killing of students. In Rosario City, several hundred students continued to demonstrate on May 22. Many trade union organizations in Rosario and Santa Fe declared a 24-hour general strike on May 23 to protest against the government atrocity and to support the just struggle of the students. Students in various parts of Venezuela continued to hold demonstrations against persecution in the past few days. In defiance of the police suppression, 1,000 students in Marcaibo took to the streets on May 22. They erected barricades and fought back at the reactionary police with stones. The demonstrators attacked the "home of Americas" which houses many offices attached to the

U.S. embassy. Student struggle also broke out in the cities of Cabimas, Merida, San Antonio and Guanare. 1,000 students in Valencia recently stage a march on the capital, Caracas, to protest against the reactionary authorities' suppression of the students. In Montevideo, capital of Uruguay, several groups of students took to the streets on May 21, to hold demonstrations in support of the Argentine students' struggle against persecution. The demonstrators shouted "Ongania, assassin!", and other slogans to protest against the killing of students by the reactionary Ongania government. The demonstrators also expressed support for the just struggle of the striking meat-packing workers in Uruguay. More than 8,000 university and middle school students in Concepcion, Chile, began a strike for an indefinite period on May 22. They demanded government acquittal of 19 workers of the "Saba" factory who had been unjustifiable charged with incendiarism and protested against them, arrest of demonstrating students. On May 20, thousands of workers and students held a demonstration and fought for several hours with the police sent to suppress them. In Santiago, the Chilean capital, groups of workers and students held successive demonstrations. They shouted slogans calling for unity between the workers and students and (demanded the acquittal of the 19 arrested workers. In Rio de Janerio, Brazil, several hundred students of the Federal University went on strike for an indefinite period to protest against the reactionary educational system and the unjustifiable dismissal of more than 60 professors by the pro-US. dictatorship.

In Tegucigalpa, capital of Honduras, students of the vocational technical institute, following their strike on May 19, held a street demonstration on May 21 in strong protest against the killing of a student by the reactionary police during the "visit" of Rockefeller. "Special envoy" of the chieftain of U.S. imperialism, Nixon. The students demanded that the assassin be severely punished. In Guayaquil, biggest city in Equador, students and stalking workers occupied the building of the University of Guayaquil in protest against the reactionary educational system. The students and workers held a demonstration to protest against the reactionary measures of the government and demanded the resignation of the Minister of the Interior and the President of the University of Guyaquil. The demonstrators shouted: "down with U.S. imperialism!" and "Universities belong to the people!" They attacked the U.S. Consulate with stones and incendiary bottles.

43. PERU MIDDLE CLASS NATIONALIZES OIL.
JUNE 21, 1969 PAGE 17

On October 8, Peru's president, Belaunde Terry was overthrown in a bloodless militarily coup by "pro-nationalist" officers angered by his refusal to nationalize Standard Oil's International Petroleum Company. The military then seized the I.P.C. holdings and demanded from the United States $1 billion worth of profits taken from the country by the I. P. C. over the past 40 years. Behind the move lies the fact of more than four decades of robbery by Rockefeller's Standard Oil. The oilfields which the militarists have recently moved to nationalize were grabbed off by Standard in the 1920. In the years following, Rockefeller acquired title to 135,000 acres of choice Peruvian land in the name of the Cerro de Pasco Corporation, and in 1964, through the agency of Chase-Manhattan Bank, bought up the 38-branch Banco Continental of Peru. Subsoil rights to the oil-bearing area of Peru were originally held by British capitalists who acquired them from a corrupt government in violation of a law prohibiting the alienation of such rights from the nation. Title was transferred to an English-owned company in Canada, International Petroleum, whose stock was later bought up by Standard Oil of New Jersey. Once before, in 1963, the Peruvian Congress moved to nationalize the oilfields but retreated when the British government, on the grounds that it had been party to the original award, and the Canadian government, on the ground that the company was "Canadian", resisted nationalization.

With Britain and Canada ready and willing to run interference for the Yankee billionaires the United States government was able to remain discretely in the background, stating only that they would accept any settlement satisfactory to the company. Now Washington finds it necessary to take direct charge, claiming that the Canadian incorporation of the company is meaningless, that the United States is the aggrieved party. (This is an interesting development in view of the claim advanced in some quarters that Canada is an imperialist country in her own right because some U. S. -owned subsidiaries handle a certain amount of overseas investments from here. When a push comes to shove, the Yankees are quick to show who is the real boss of the show.) When Belaunde Terry made some quite modest demands on Standard and other interests, amounting to no more than a request for payment of back taxes, the United States, aided by Britain, put pressure on his government. Belaunde finally capitulated to the pressure and exonerated the company completely from paying any back debts to Peru. Just as in all Latin American countries, living conditions for the Peruvian working people are absolutely deplorable. Unemployment, starvation, "homes" constructed of cardboard and tin, tens of thousands of sick and hungry people huddled into the poverty ghettoes known as "barrios", than rim the cities like Lima, and landless peasants who own not even a patch of soil on which to grow a few vegetables, even as Yankee land-grabbers carve out virtual kingdoms for themselves. The already unbelievably horrible conditions of the people grow daily worse while a few foreign investors reap untold wealth from the tortured land. A relative handful of traitor puppets have been content to sell-out the country's natural resource and act as overseers and hangmen for U. S. imperialists. The payments made to this traitor class are invested abroad, against the day when they will have to flee the wrath of the people. Resentment against these conditions, arising from foreign domination and exploitation, has been intensifying over the years to the point where workers and peasants have mounted sharp struggle against the imperialist exploiters and the regime of national betrayal. The only response of the imperialists to date has been a demand for more repressive measures and an increase of taxes on the Peruvian people to provide still move facilities for the exploiters and to pay the expenses of the state bureaucracy. Given the conditions that exist in Peru it is inevitable that the middle class and the lower ranks of the national bourgeoisie would be squeezed economically and become resentful toward the regime, particularly since they are not allowed a share of the profits of national betrayal. These groups entertain desires to transform the administration into one that more closely represents their class interests. Out they carefully avoid mobilization of the masses and revolution. Rather than chance an appeal to the working people, they will seek means to achieve their ends by "peaceful and orderly methods" if the opportunity should present itself. And in Peru the opportunity did, indeed, come to hand. The officer corp of the armed forces is manned mainly by members of those dissatisfied elements and when the crisis in the semicolonial economy becomes sharp enough they tend to side with the class group from which they sprang--especially if there appears to be real hope of success. In Peru conditions were ripe for this type of action and the army was able to organize a coup that completely avoided any appeal to the mass of the people. Instead, the militarists use the visit of some Russian warships and hastily-signed trade agreements with Russia's eastern European colonies to try to bolster their image of "national independence" from U. S. imperialism. But without a mass base the army administration cannot last. "The internal contradictions that tear apart the various elements that support the dictatorship will cause it to break up from within, and U. S. pressure front without--including armed intervention if deemed necessary--will hasten the development of the internal factors. The army administration will quite soon be confronted with the choice of mobilizing the masses for revolutionary anti-imperialist resistance, or of coming to terms with the foreign exploiters, which will mean capitulation. Being exploiters themselves, and panic-stricken at the idea of armed revolution, it is a foregone conclusion that this administration as presently constituted, will choose the path of capitulation to the imperialists. The fight for national independence in Peru will make real advances only when the working people take over the leadership of the anti-imperialist forces.

44. Swedish Government Supports U.S. Aggression. July 19, 1969 Page 9.

The Swedish government has never advocated a righteous Vietnam policy. Sometimes we are allowed to hear some beautiful government words. But in practice the government has often supported the U.S. imperialism directly. Therefore we must increase our support to the NLF and combat U.S. imperialism.

In a speech January 18, 1965, the Swedish foreign minister Torsten Nilsson said: "We miss the suppositions to judge safely if the American tactics conduct the raised objectives."

Which were the tactics? Continued murdering and escalation of the aggression in Vietnam. The objectives? The U.S. government talked about peace and lied about "aggression from the North". Why should "we" not be able to "judge" and condemn this? "In the Vietnam conflict it is hard to determine to what degree the participants have support for their activity in international treaties and folkjudical rules."

What does Torsten Nilsson mean by "activity"? The U.S "activity" was an aggressive war and the "activity" of the Vietnamese was a defense struggle. Which international treaties and folkjudical rules support an aggressive war and condemn resistance

165

fight? "The thing that has upset the Swedish public most during recent months are the increasing number of testimonies about terror and mass reprisals used by both sides in Vietnam. The government shares the Swedish people's disgust for terror activities and reprisal methods, however they are motivated."

Torsten Nilsson does not distinguish between aggressor and victim. Did the "terror and mass reprisals" used by e.g. the Norwegian resistance fighters against the Nazi occupants and their Norwegian puppets during the Second World War also disgust the Swedish minister of foreign affairs? Victims of aggression always have the rights to defend themselves with all possible means. This was only three short quotations from the minister of foreign affairs in 1965. But they show clearly the government's attitude in basic questions: it refuses consistently to take a stand against the US imperialists aggressive war and for the Vietnamese just resistance struggle. This implies nothing else but a support to the United States. And those that have given their wholehearted support to the NLF-- the Vietnam demonstrators-have been condemned in reactionary statement. About 200 have been sentenced to pay fines. Recently a NLF activist was sentenced to jail. December 20, 1967 in Stockholm the police, blessed by the government attacked a demonstration for support to the NLF, Many were mishandled. The government tried as long as possible to stop the Russel Tribunal from being held in Sweden-the same Tribunal that demasked many US war crimes in Vietnam. Prime Minister Tage Erlander said that the Tribunal did not further peace in Vietnam.

The government helps make the US imperialist policy possible by supporting the US dollar, which has been weakened by the same imperialist policy: military bases all over the world, military support to dozens of reactionary regimes, etc. The government even refuses to give a statement about SENTAB and other Swedish enterprises, that give direct support to the US war in South East Asia. The government refuses to give asylum to the Vietnam War Refusers seeking refuge in Sweden. In this way it "escapes" taking a stand to the US war. All these acts against the Vietnamese people's struggle have been blended with halfhearted statements supporting the NLF, The government have swayed to and fro in the Vietnam question since 1965. Its last "stand" was taken in the parliament foreign affairs debate recently. Torsten Nilsson then informed that the Swedish government will present the DRV with fertilizers worth 10 million Swedish Kronor. He "hoped" that South Vietnam would be included in the aid program, "but as long as the bombing goes in South Vietnam it is useless to give any help". Also now Torsten Nilsson refuses to take any stand. The bombs do not fall by themselves. For years they have been dropped at the command of the U.S. imperialists. But the government pretends knowing nothing about it. Thus we can see that the government now as before conducts a means. policy of support to the US imperialists. Of course the government has taken some positive stands; the recognition of the DRV, permission for the NLF information office in Stockholm. But these decisions were not taken by the government on its own initiative; it has been forced by the firm public opinion. We cannot expect the government to act differently in the future. Therefore we must continue the work for solidarity with the Vietnamese people and increase the support to the NLF. The United NLF-groups of Sweden.

45. BOSTON PURGE. JULY 19, 1969 PAGE 13

As of May 24, 1969 these renegade, cultural nationalist opportunists are no longer members of the Black Panther Party. The Boston branch of the Black Panther Party has affirmed anew the discipline of the Party and has purged these fools from the Party ranks for the reasons stated below

1. Failure to follow the teachings of Minister of Defense, Huey P. Newton
2. For complete disregard for the discipline of the Party.
3. Subjectivism
4. Opportunism against the people.
5. Propagating cultural nationalist madness inside the Party instead of class struggle.
5. Racism
6. Individualism

The following people have been purged:

1. Chico Neblett, Field Marshall
2. T.D.Pawley, Asst to the Field Marshall
3. Delano Farrar, Area Captain
4. Frank Hughes, Lt. of Information
5. Karen Flippen, Lt. of Finance
6. Kay Glaspy, Communications Secretary
7. Rene Neblett, Lt. of Culture
8. Yazid Nzinga, section leader
9. Mike Claytor, subsection leader.
10. Paula Firmin
11. Les Wood
12. Monica Millet
13. Mike Grattan
14. Roger Freeman
15. Bernadette Mount
16. Pamela Hayes
17. Maurice Kalhman

In May of this year a bunch of cultural nationalist fools lead by Chico Neblett attempted to undermine the people's revolution. These pea-brained counter-revolutionaries tried to go against the teachings of the Minister of Defense and take over the Boston Branch of the Black Panther Party. They failed in their attempt and were purged from the party. Chico joined the party with the other bootlicker Stokely

Carmichael, ever since that time he has been steadily robbing the people. His 1969 Corvett, his fur coat, and his expensive camera equipment can prove that Chico was going around talking about some madness he called Pan-Africanism. All it really was, though, was a bunch of bullshit to hide the robbing of the people he has been doing. By going against the teachings of Huey P. Newton, Chico has said "fuck the people, fuck the Party, and the complete and total liberation of blacks here in fascist America."

All Power To The People
The Remaining Members Of The Boston Branch,
Black Panther Party

46. Field Marshall Don Cox
At The Conference. July 26, 1969. Page 11

(United Front Against Fascism conference) All Power To The People! You can do better than that. All Power to the people! Right on! Huey P. Newton says, "Any unarmed people are slaves, or are subject to slavery at any given moment. If the guns are taken out of the hands of the people and only the pigs have guns, then it's off to the concentration camps, the gas chambers, or whatever the fascists in America come up with. One of the democratic rights of the United States, the Second Amendment to the Constitution, gives the people the right to bear arms. However, there is a greater right; the right of human dignity that gives all men the right to defend themselves." As the black liberation struggle in the United States developed from a lower to a higher level, from a lunch counter sit-in in Alabama to guerrilla type actions all across the United States, we saw and we see the demagogues beginning their campaign against 'crime in the streets.' We see the demagogues mobilizing supporters, the forces of fascism under the philosophy of 'law and order,' the guise under which fascism is growing in America. Backing up the rhetoric of the demagogue is the "beefing up" of the gestapo pig police forces all across America. In addition, more and more gun control legislation, the guise under which the people are being unarmed, is being passed every day to take away the democratic right to bear arms, which in turn dehumanizes you by preventing you from exercising your human right to self-defense.

Eldridge Cleaver said, "The oppressor has no rights that the oppressed are bound to respect." Because those people that own and control the institutions of finance capital, the Rockefellers, the Kennedys, the Hunts, etc., want to maintain their control because they want to maintain the oppression and exploitation of mankind. They do not have the right to dispatch their fascist troops through the cities of America to brutalize and murder to maintain their terror over the people. The only way they can exercise their right to oppress and exploit you is if you give up your right to human dignity, and do not defend yourself. We, the members of the Black Panther Party, say there is an alternative to fighting racism, other than with more racism. We say the way to fight racism is with solidarity. We also say the only alternative to the violence perpetrated against the people by the fascist troops of finance capital or slavery, is revolution. Many people throughout America have not decided or even dealt with how they're gonna deal with the power of finance capital as manifested in those fascist pig police forces. But, black people, unorganized, have shown through the many rebellions that they ain't goin' for it. Huey P. Newton didn't for it. The Black Panther Party ain't goin' for it. Los Siete de la Raza didn't go for it. You'd better make up your minds quick. Because [ ] don't see much time left. Black people in general, may not relate to the word, or the definitions of fascism as articulated by Dimitrov but black people sure relate to the social practice of 400 years of brutality and murder perpetrated on us by the fathers of fascism. Huey P. Newton says, "racist dog police must withdraw from the black community, or face the wrath of the armed people. The Black Panther Party has a motto. It is a quote by Chairman Mao Tse Tung of the Chinese Communist Party, "We are advocates of the abolition of war. We do not want war, but war can only be abolished through war. In order to get rid of the gun it is necessary to pick up the gun."

Power To The People!

47. THE PLP VS. THE PEOPLE.
AUGUST 2, 1969 PAGE 9

First of all, thanks to the Black Panther Party for making the First U.F.A.F. possible; and then I want to say to all the beautiful people who were there: "Power to the People" and let's get out there and put it all into practice.

To those who attended the U.F.A.F. conference, the conference represented not only the first constructive plan for action against Fascism, but it was also a beautiful, unique thing in this respect: more than 1,000 people from many different geographical locations and many different lines of ideological theories were together in unity against a common enemy: fascism. They were made aware, if not already aware, of the enemy and laid petty arguments and ideological struggle aside and tried instead to deal with the one common big problem: fascism.

To those people who had been wondering why the PLP was expelled from the SDS, it became increasingly clear. PLP, instead of working against the enemy, had aligned itself with the pigs and was trying to work against the people. PLP tried to disrupt the U.F.A.F conference by passing out leaflets against the holding of the conference and against the vanguard party, by distorting facts just as the pig "news media" does, and by lying to the people. After asking one of these fools what the basis was for passing out leaflets against the people's United Front, his reply was: "The PLP doesn't believe the Panthers know what Fascism is." Since even "apolitical" people know that the Panthers are being terrorized and brutalized; and since the vanguard party has felt Fascism's foul boot on its back more than any other group of people, his reply was not only stupid, it was oinking in the faces of the people. In the midst of speeches a few instigators would now and then seek to disrupt the conference-yelling, telling people to walk out, etc. To those who had never heard of the PLP before, and were now aware of its existence, their reaction to PLP was not favorable, to say the least. They condemned the PLP and started to seek out more information about PLP and soon found out and understood why the SDS expelled them from its ranks:

1) PLP not only refused to support the Vietnam N.L.F. and its struggles to liberate the people, but also attacked the N.L.F and the Revolutionary Government of Cuba, 2) On the campuses, PLP opposes most black student struggles. It opposed demands for increased black studies programs and admissions, but put forth a resolution advocating preferential hiring of minority non-academic "help," i.e., maids and janitors --where these minorities are already preferentially hired. This shows that PLP has an attitude of bigotry and "white supremacy" and a lack of understanding, and thereby a racist attitude; a slave-master-slave attitude as medieval and as foul as any Ku Klux Klanner. 3) PLP has led unprincipled attacks on the Black Panther Party and the League of Revolutionary Black Workers. In leading these attacks they have lied to the people

branding the Panthers as racists and saying that the Panthers have "no class outlook and believe they are out to fight a war against white people in general." Since this is obviously untrue, even to many who didn't attend the conference, as far as most people are concerned, not only are the PLPers sadly miseducated, uneducated, or whatever, but since they, in their actions, so closely resemble the lying pig news media there can be a direct line of similarity drawn between the PLP and the pigs. Indeed, they can be classified as pigs and charged with being enemies of the people. Stupid as they may be and as absurd as their warped statements are, the PLP means to be just as harmful to the interests of the people as any lying, oinking, foul, pig politician; greedy, avaricious businessman; or murderous, brutalizing pig would be. But the PLP's squeals grow weaker and weaker as the people are now hip to their slimy snakelike tactics. The PLP not only failed to disrupt the U.F.A.F., they were ignored for the most part. The people were there to learn and work together on important issues; they knew they were not there to listen to absurd oinkings from the mouths of fools. By slithering in and out of the conference all the PLPers accomplished by their actions was that they exposed their true nature to the people: that as lying, snakelike enemies of the people disguised as representing the true interests of the people. Well, enough of the PLP and all other petty, insignificant, worthless, brainless and warped so-called "progressive" parties like the PLP. The enemies of the people shall be dealt with by the people, for there are more people than there are pigs.

Down With Fascism. Power To The People. Power To The Panther Vanguard.

Carole

48. Message To Revolutionary Women.
August 9. Page 23

Black Women, Black Women, Hold your head up, and look ahead. We too are needed in the revolution.

We too are strong. We too are a threat to the oppressive enemy. We are revolutionaries. We are the other half of our revolutionary men. We are their equal halves, may it be with gun in hand, or battling in streets to make this country a socialist lead. Sisters, let's educate our people. Combat liberalism, and combat male chauvinism. Awaken our men to the fact that we are no more nor no less than they. We are as revolutionary as they. For too long, we have been alone. For far too long we have been women without men, for far too long we have been double oppressed, not only by the capitalist society, but also by our men. Now we are no longer alone, our men are by our sides. We revolutionary men and women are the halves of each other. We must continue to educate our men, and bring their minds from a male chauvinistic level to a higher level. Our men need, want and will love the beautiful children, that come from our fruitful wombs. They need our trust and encouragement as well as we need theirs. They need us to educate, them, the people and our children as well as we need them to educate us. Sisters, we are being called by life itself. We are being called by the revolution. We are mothers of revolutionaries, with us is the future of our people. We my sisters, are mothers of revolution and within our wombs is the army of the people. Sisters! Revolution Is Here! Bring Forth The Army! Bring Forth the Guns! We my sisters are revolutionary women of revolutionary men! We are mothers of revolution! Comrade Candi Robinson

49. THE BLACK PANTHER: MIRROR OF THE PEOPLE. JANUARY 17, 1970

Just what is the Black Panther Black Community News Service? Is it something like the bourgeois press, to be read once and then discarded in the nearest trash can, or is it something else--something more? The Black Panther Black Community News Service, is not just a newspaper in the traditional sense of the word, it's more than that.

The Black Panther Black Community News Service is a living contemporary history of our people's struggle for liberation at the grass roots level. It's something to be studied and grasped, and saved for future generations to read, learn and understand. The Black Panther Black Community News Service tells the story of our people's struggle in the streets. Its story unfolds far from the perfumed parlors of the petty bourgeoisie. It tells the true story of what happens in the concrete inner-city jungles of Babylon when brothers and sisters off the block, workers, and members of the petty bourgeoisie decide to cast aside their petty personal goals and aspirations, and begin to work unselfishly together with a common goal in mind: to serve the people and liberate the colony, by the only means necessary--the GUN. The history of the Black

Panther Black Community News Service, goes back to the first issue printed in 1967 (Vol. I No.1), back to the vicious murder of Denzil Dowell by fascist gestapo pigs in Richmond, Calif., and documents what happens when the people of the community say "this is enough," decide to arm themselves to put an end to exploitation and oppression and is an objective lesson in the art of self-defense, serving the people, national liberation, and revolution. The Black Panther documents step by step the actions taken by, and programs instituted by the Black Panther Party in its unstoppable drive to serve the people; and documents before the whole world the repression and murders committed by Amerikkka's corrupt monopoly capital in its dastardly attempts to stop this move to institute people's power. The Black Panther Black Community News Service, tells how our courageous Minister of Defense, Huey P. Newton, the baddest brother to ever step into history, stood up in the bowels of fascist Amerikkka with a shotgun in his hands and told those murderous mad dogs who occupy our community like a foreign army: "My name is Huey P. Newton, Minister of Defense of the Black Panther Party. I'm standing on my constitutional right to bear arms to defend my people. If you shoot at me pig, I'm shooting back." And thus his courageous example moved the struggle of our people to a higher level--from throwing rocks and bottles, to arming themselves for survival. The Black Panther teaches the people the strategic means for resisting the power structure. The Black Panther Black Community News Service, tells how the correct examples of the Party, led by Huey P. Newton, spread like wildfire throughout fascist Amerikkka--as exemplified by Detroit and Newark--and how on the morning of October 28, 1967, two night-riding greasy Oakland pigs tried to murder our Minister of Defense from ambush. It also tells how that attempt failed and one pig, Frey went to the pig sty in the sky, and the other one, Haines, somehow received three bullet holes.

The Black Panther documents for all humanity to see, how the wretched slaves of Amerikkka moved fearlessly to establish All Power To The People. It also shows how the forces of re-action perfected their ambushes and murdered Li'l Bobby, Robert, Tommy, Steve and other Party members in attempts to stop us. The weekly issues of The Black Panther also shows how people who will be free refuse to be either cowed or intimidated by death, imprisonment or exile, and continue to develop and expand. It is a lesson in the objective truth, that the spirit of the people is indeed greater than the man's technology. The best that humanity possesses will never yield to any oppressor. Issue by issue the people's revolutionary struggle for national salvation unfolds in the pages of The Black Panther Community News Service, free from the dis-tortion, bias, and lies of the oppressor controlled mass me-dia. The People's paper tells how starting out with nothing, the People's Party, The Black Panther Party, moved with the people to implement Free Breakfast Programs to feed our hungry children, Free Health Clinics to care for the sick, Free Clothing Programs to clothe our needy, Liberation Schools to educate our youth, and Community Centers to keep the community informed; and how with each meal served, with each child clothed, and with each bandage applied, we were attacked wilder and wilder--Fred Hampton and Mark Clark murdered in their sleep by Chicago's thin blue line on December 4, 1969 and the L.A. office attacked by 400 crazed pigs on December 8, 1969 (Vol. Iv No.2). The Black Panther Black Community News Service, is not only a history of the people's growth, but also the pigs' fanatical repression as they near total destruction. The Black Panther documents and indicts Amerikkka for the fascist police state that it is, attempting to crush all dissent by force. The Black Panther Black Community News Service, when put together is a glorious living history, a testament to the fact that no matter how the pigs try to stop us, the people will be free; clearly points out that all the wild attacks by the pigs is like a fool picking up a rock only to drop it on his own foot; and gives proof of the objective truth that oppression only creates resistance. The Black Panther Black Community News Service, is a living, breathing history that continues each and every day. Each new issue has its message, its lessons to be learned, its objective truth. No! The Black Panther Black Community News Service, is not an ordinary newspaper. It is the flesh and blood, the sweat and tears of our people. It is a continuation of the story of the middle passage, of Denmark Vesey, of Nat Turner, of Harriet Tubman, of Malcolm X, and countless other oppressed people who put freedom and dignity beyond personal gain. The Black Panther Black Community News Service, is truly a mirror of the spirit of the people.

All Power To The People Pow's For Panthers Black Panther Party Political Prisoner, Denver Colorado Landon Williams - *The Black Panther*, January 17, 1970

50. On the Ideology of the Black Panther Party.
   Pamphlet, 1970

Eldridge Cleaver – Minister of Information, Black Panther Party
The following article introduces a new series of articles on the ideology of the Black Panther Party by our Minister of Information, Eldridge Cleaver.

> "One of the great contributions of Huey P. Newton is that he gave the Black Panther Party a firm ideological foundation that frees us from ideological flunkeyism and open (sic) up the path to the future."

Eldridge Cleaver Minister of Information Black Panther Party U.S.A. We have said: the ideology of the Black Panther Party is the historical experience of Black people and the wisdom gained by Black people in their 400 year long struggle against the system of racist oppression and economic exploitation in Babylon, interpreted through the prism of the Marxist-Leninist analysis by our Minister of Defense, Huey P. Newton. However, we must place heavy emphasis upon the last part of that definition — 'interpreted ... by our Minister of Defense..'. the world of Marxism-Leninism has become a jungle of opinion in which conflicting interpretations, from Right Revisionism to Left Dogmatism, foist off their reactionary and blind philosophies as revolutionary Marxism-Leninism. Around the world and in every nation people, all who call themselves Marxist-Leninists, are at each other's throats. Such a situation presents serious problems to a young party, such as ours, that is still in the process of refining its ideology. When we say that we are Marxist-Leninists, we mean that we have studied and understood the classical principles of scientific socialism and that we have adapted these principles to our own situation for ourselves. However, we do not move with a closed mind to new ideas or information. At the same time, we know that we must rely upon our own brains in solving ideological problems as they relate to us. For too long Black people have relied upon the analyses and ideological perspectives of others. Our struggle has reached a point now where it would be absolutely suicidal for us to continue this posture of dependency. No other people in the world are in the same position as we are, and no other people in the world can get us out of it except ourselves. There are those who are all too willing to do our thinking for us, even if it gets us killed. However, they are not willing to follow through and do our dying for us. If thoughts bring about our deaths, let them at least be our own thoughts, so that we will have broken, once and for all, with the flunkeyism of dying for every cause and every error—except our own. One of the great contributions of Huey P. Newton is that he gave the Black Panther Party a firm ideological foundation that frees us from ideological flunkeyism and opens up the path to the future—a future to which we must provide new ideological formulations to fit our ever changing situation. Much – most—of the teachings of Huey P. Newton are unknown to the people because Huey has been placed in a position where it is impossible to really communicate with us. And much that he taught while he was free has gotten distorted and watered down precisely because the Black Panther Party has been too hung up in relating to the courts and trying to put on a good face in order to help lawyers convince juries of the justice of our cause. This whole court hang-up has created much confusion. For instance, many people confuse the Black Panther Party with the Free Huey Movement or the many other mass activities that we have been forced to indulge in in order to build mass support for our comrades who have gotten captured by the pigs. We are absolutely correct in indulging in such mass activity. But we are wrong when we confuse our mass line with our party line. Essentially, what Huey did was to provide the ideology and the methodology for organizing the Black Urban Lumpenproletariat. Armed with this ideological perspective and method, Huey transformed the Black lumpenproletariat from the forgotten people at the bottom of society into the vanguard of the proletariat. There is a lot of confusion over whether we are members of the Working Class or whether we are Lumpenproletariat. It is necessary to confront this confusion, because it has a great deal to do with the strategy and tactics that we follow and with our strained relations with the White radicals from the oppressor section of Babylon.

Some so-called Marxist-Leninists will attack us for what we have to say, but that is a good thing and not a bad thing because some people call themselves Marxist-Leninists who are downright enemies of Black people. Later for them. We want them to step boldly forward, as they will do— blinded by their own stupidity and racist arrogance—that it will be easier for us to deal with them in the future. We make these criticisms in a fraternal spirit of how some Marxist-Leninists apply the classical principles to the specific situation that exists in the United States because we believe in the need for a unified revolutionary movement in the United States, a movement that is informed by the revolutionary principles of scientific socialism. Huey P. Newton says that "power is the ability to define phenomena and make it act in a desired manner." And we need power, desperately, to counter the power of the pigs that now bears so heavily upon us. Ideology is a comprehensive definition of a status quo that takes into account both the history and the future of that status quo and serves as the social glue that holds a people together and through which a people relate to the world and other groups of people in the world. The correct ideology is an invincible weapon against the oppressor in our struggle for freedom and liberation. Marx defined the epoch of the bourgeoisie and laid bare the direction of the Proletarian future. He analyzed Capitalism and defined the method of its doom: Violent revolution by the proletariat against the bourgeois state apparatus of class oppression and repression. Revolutionary violence against the counter-revolutionary class violence perpetrated through the special repressive force of the armed tentacles (sic.) Of the state. This great definition by Marx and Engels became the mightiest weapon in the hands of oppressed people in the history of ideology. It marks a gigantic advance for all mankind. And since Marx's time, his definition has been strengthened, further elaborated, illumined, and further refined. But Marxism has never really dealt with the United States of America. There have been some very nice attempts. People have done the best that they know how. However, in the past, Marxist-Leninists in the United States have relied too heavily upon foreign, imported analyses and have seriously distorted the realities of the American scene. We might say that the Marxism-Leninism of the past belongs to the gestation period of Marxism-Leninism in the United States, and that now is the time when a new, strictly American ideological synthesis will arise, spring up from the hearts and souls of the oppressed people inside Babylon, and uniting these people and hurling them mightily, from the force of their struggle, into the future. The swiftly developing revolution in America is like the gathering of a mighty storm, and nothing can stop that storm from finally bursting, inside America, washing away the pigs of the power structure and all their foul, oppressive works. And the children of the pigs and the oppressed people will dance and spit upon the common graves of these pigs. There are some Black people in the United States who are absolutely happy, who do not feel themselves to be oppressed, and who think that they are free. Some even believe that the President wouldn't lie, and that he is more or less an honest man; that Supreme Court decisions were almost written by god in person; that the Police are Guardians of the Law; and that people who do not have jobs are just plain lazy and good-for-nothing and should be severely punished. These are like crabs that must be left to boil a little longer in the post of oppression before they will be ready and willing to relate. But the overwhelming majority of Black people are uptight, know that they are oppressed and not free; and they wouldn't believe Nixon if he confessed to being a pig; they don't relate to the Supreme Court or any other court; and they know that the racist pig cops are their sworn enemies. As for poverty, they know what that is all about. These millions of Black people have no political representation, they are unorganized, and they do not own or control any of the natural resources; they neither own nor control any of the industrial machinery, and their daily life is a hustle to make it by any means necessary in the struggle to survive. Every Black person knows that the wind may change at any given moment and that Lynch Mob, made up of White members of the "Working Class", might come breathing down his neck if not kicking down his door. It is because of these factors that when we begin to talk about being Marxist-Leninists, we must be very careful to make it absolutely clear just what we are talking about. On the subject of racism, Marxism-Leninism offers us very little assistance. In fact, there is much evidence that Marx and Engels were themselves racists--just like their White brothers and sisters of their era, and just as many Marxist-Leninists of our own time are also racists. Historically, Marxism-Leninism has been an outgrowth of European problems and it has been primarily preoccupied with finding solutions to European problems. With the founding of the Democratic People's Republic of Korea in 1948 and the People's Republic of China in 1949, something new was injected into Marxism-Leninism, and it ceased to be just a narrow, exclusively European phenomenon. Comrade Kim Il Sung and Comrade Mao Tse-tung applied the classical principles of

Marxism-Leninism to the conditions in their own countries and thereby made the ideology into something useful for their people. But they rejected that part of the analysis that was not beneficial to them and had only to do with the welfare of Europe. Given the racist history of the United States, it is very difficult for Black people to comfortably call themselves Marxist-Leninists or anything else that takes its name from White people. It's like praying to Jesus, a White man. We must emphasize the fact that Marx and Lenin didn't invent Socialism. They only added their contributions, enriching the doctrine, just as many others did before them and after them. And we must remember that Marx and Lenin didn't organize the Black Panther Party. Huey P. Newton and Bobby Seale did. Not until we reach Fanon do we find a major Marxist-Leninist theoretician who was primarily concerned about the problems of Black people, wherever they may be found. And even Fanon, in his published works, was primarily focused on Africa. It is only indirectly that his works are beneficial to Afro-Americans. It is just easier to relate to Fanon because he is clearly free of that racist bias that blocks out so much about the Black man in the hands of Whites who are primarily interested in themselves and the problems of their own people. But even though we are able to relate heavily to Fanon, he has not given us the last word on applying the Marxist-Leninist analysis to our problems inside the United States. No one is going to do this for us because no one can. We have to do it ourselves, and until we do, we are going to be uptight. We must take the teachings of Huey P. Newton as our foundation and go from there. Any other course will bring us to a sorry and regrettable end. Fanon delivered a devastating attack upon Marxism-Leninism for its narrow preoccupation with Europe and the affairs and salvation of White folks, while lumping all third world peoples into the category of Lumpenproletariat and then forgetting them there; Fanon unearthed the category of the Lumpenproletariat and began to deal with it, recognizing that vast majorities of the colonized people fall into that category. It is because of the fact that Black people in the United States are also colonized that Fanon's analysis is so relevant to us. After studying Fanon, Huey P. Newton and Bobby Seale began to apply his analysis of colonized people to Black people in the United States. They adopted the Fanonian perspective, but they gave it a uniquely Afro-American content. Just as we must make the distinctions between the mother country and the colony when dealing with Black people and White people as a whole, we must also make this distinction when we deal with the categories of Working Class and Lumpenproletariat. We have, in the United States, a "Mother Country Working Class" and a "Working Class from the Black Colony". We also have a Mother Country Lumpenproletariat and a Lumpenproletariat from the Black Colony. Inside the Mother Country, these categories are fairly stable, but when we look at the Black Colony, we find that the hard and fast distinctions melt away. This is because of the leveling effect of the colonial process and the fact that all Black people are colonized, even if some of them occupy favored positions in the schemes of the Mother Country colonizing exploiters. There is a difference between the problems of the Mother Country Working Class and the Working Class from the Black Colony. There is also a difference between the Mother Country

Lumpen and the Lumpen from the Black Colony. We have nothing to gain from trying to smooth over these differences as though they don't exist, because they are objective facts that must be dealt with. To make this point clear, we have only to look at the long and bitter history of the struggles of Black Colony Workers fighting for democracy inside Mother Country Labor Unions. Historically, we have fallen into the trap of criticizing mother country labor unions and workers for the racism as an explanation for the way they treat Black workers. Of course, they are racist, but this is not the full explanation. White workers belong to a totally different world than that of Black workers. They are caught up in a totally different economic, political, and social reality, and on the basis of this distinct reality, the pigs of the power structure and treacherous labor leaders find it very easy to manipulate them with Babylonian racism. This complex reality presents us with many problems, and only through proper analysis can these problems be solved. The lack of a proper analysis is responsible for the ridiculous approach to these problems that we find among Mother Country Marxist-Leninists. And their improper analysis leads them to advocate solutions that are doomed to failure in advance. The key area of the confusion has to do with falsely assuming the existence of one All-American Proletariat; one All-American Working Class; and one All-American Lumpenproletariat.

O.K. We are Lumpen. Right on. The Lumpenproletariat are all those who have no secure relationship or vested interest in the means of production and the institutions of capitalist society. That part of the "Industrial Reserve Army" held perpetually in reserve; who have never worked and never will;

who can't find a job; who are unskilled and unfit; who have been displaced by machines, automation, and cybernation, and were never "retained or invested with new skills"; all those on Welfare or receiving State Aid. Also, the so-called "Criminal Element", those who live by their wits, existing off that which they rip off, who stick guns in the faces of businessmen and say 'stick'em up', or 'give it up'! Those who don't even want a job, who hate to work and can't relate to punching some pig's time clock, who would rather punch a pig in the mouth and rob him than punch that same pig's time clock and work for him, those whom Huey P. Newton calls "the illegitimate capitalists". In short, all those who simply have been locked out of the economy and robbed of their rightful social heritage. But even though we are Lumpen, we are still members of the Proletariat, a category which theoretically cuts across national boundaries but which in practice leaves something to be desired.

Contradictions within the Proletariat of the USA
In both the Mother Country and the Black Colony, the Working Class is the Right Wing of the Proletariat, and the Lumpenproletariat is the Left Wing. Within the Working Class itself, we have a major contradiction between the Unemployed and the Employed. And we definitely have a major contradiction between the Working Class and the Lumpen. Some blind so-called Marxist-Leninists accuse the Lumpen of being parasites upon the Working Class. This is a stupid charge derived from reading too many of Marx's footnotes and taking some of his offhand scurrilous remarks for holy writ. In reality, it is accurate to say that the Working Class,

particularly the American Working Class, is a parasite upon the heritage of mankind, of which the Lumpen has been totally robbed by the rigged system of Capitalism which in turn, has thrown the majority of mankind upon the junkheap while it buys off a percentage with jobs and security. The Working Class that we must deal with today shows little resemblance to the Working Class of Marx's day. In the days of its infancy, insecurity, and instability, the Working Class was very revolutionary and carried forward the struggle against the bourgeoisie. But through long and bitter struggles, the Working Class has made some inroads into the Capitalist system, carving out a comfortable niche for itself. The advent of Labor Unions, Collective Bargaining, the Union Shop, Social Security, and other special protective legislation has castrated the Working Class, transforming it into the bought-off Labor Movement--a most un-revolutionary, reformist minded movement that is only interested in higher wages and more job security. The Labor Movement has abandoned all basic criticism of the Capitalist system of exploitation itself. The George Meanys, Walter Reuthers, and A. Phillip Randolphs may correctly be labelled traitors to the proletariat as a whole, but they accurately reflect and embody the outlook and aspirations of the Working Class. The Communist Party of the United States of America, at its poorly attended meetings, may raise the roof with its proclamations of being the Vanguard of the Working Class, but the Working Class itself looks upon the Democratic Party as the legitimate vehicle of its political salvation. As a matter of fact, the Working Class of our time has become a new industrial elite, resembling more the chauvanistic elites of the selfish craft and trade guilds of

Marx's time than the toiling masses ground down in abject poverty. Every job on the market in the American Economy today demands as high a complexity of skills as did the jobs in the elite trade and craft guilds of Marx's time. In a highly mechanized economy, it cannot be said that the fantastically high productivity is the product solely of the Working Class. Machines and computers are not members of the Working Class, although some spokesmen for the Working Class, particularly some Marxist-Leninists, seem to think like machines and computers. The flames of revolution, which once raged like an inferno in the heart of the Working Class, in our day have dwindled into a flickering candle light, only powerful enough to bounce the Working Class back and forth like a ping pong ball between the Democratic Party and the the Republican Party every four years, never once even glancing at the alternatives on the Left.

Who speaks for the Lumpen Proletariat?
Some Marxist-Leninists are guilty of that class egotism and hypocrisy often displayed by superior classes to those beneath them on the social scale. On the one hand, they freely admit that their organizations are specifically designed to represent the interests of the Working Class. But then they go beyond that to say that by representing the interests of the Working Class, they represent the interests of the Proletariat as a whole. This is clearly not true. This is a fallacious assumption based upon the egotism of these organizations and is partly responsible for their miserable failure to make a revolution in Babylon. And since there clearly is a contradiction between the right wing and the left wing of

the Proletariat, just as the right wing has created its own organizations, it is necessary for the left wing to have its form of organization to represent its interests against all hostile classes--including the Working Class. The contradiction between the Lumpen and the Working Class is very serious because it even dictates a different strategy and set of tactics. The students focus their rebellions on the campuses, and the Working Class focuses its rebellions on the factories and picket lines. But the Lumpen finds itself in the peculiar position of being unable to find a job and therefore is unable to attend the Universities. The Lumpen has no choice but to manifest its rebellion in the University of the Streets.

It's very important to recognize that the streets belong to the Lumpen, and that it is in the streets that Lumpen will make their rebellion. One outstanding characteristic of the liberation struggle of Black people in the United States has been that most of the activity has taken place in the streets. This is because, by and large, the rebellions have been been spear-headed by Black Lumpen. It is because of the Black people's lumpen relationship to the means of production and the institutions of the society that they are unable to manifest their rebellion around those means of production and institutions. But this does not mean that the rebellions that take place in the streets are not legitimate expressions of an oppressed people. These are the means of rebellion left open to the Lumpen. The Lumpen have been locked outside of the economy. And when the Lumpen does engage in direct action against the system of oppression, it is often greeted by hoots and howls from the spokesmen of the Working Class in chorus with the mouthpieces of the bourgeoisie. These talkers

199

like to put down the struggles of the Lumpen as being "spontaneous" (perhaps because they themselves did not order the actions!), "unorganized", and "chaotic and undirected". But these are only prejudiced analyses made from the narrow perspective of the Working Class. But the Lumpen moves anyway, refusing to be straight-jacketed or controlled by the tactics dictated by the conditions of life and the relationship to the means of production of the Working Class. The Lumpen finds itself in the position where it is very difficult for it to manifest its complaints against the system. The Working Class has the possibility of calling a strike against the factory and the employer and through the mechanism of Labor Unoins they can have some arbitration or some process through which its grievances are manifested. Collective bargaining is the way out of the pit of oppression and exploitation discovered by the Working Class, but the Lumpen has no opportunity to do any collective bargaining. The Lumpen has no institutionalized focus in Capitalist society. It has not immediate oppressor except perhaps the Pig Police with which it is confronted daily. So that the very conditions of life of the Lumpen dictates the so-called spontaneous reactions against the system, and because the Lumpen is in this extremely oppressed condition, it therefore has an extreme reaction against the system as a whole. It sees itself as being bypassed by all of the organizations, even by the Labor Unions, and even by the Communist Parties that despise it and look down upon it and consider it to be, in the words of Karl Marx, the father of Communist Parties, "The Scum Layer of the Society". The Lumpen is forced to create its own forms of rebellion that are consistent with its condition in life and with its relationship to the means of production and the institutions of society. That is, to strike out at all the structures around it, including at the reactionary Right Wing of the Proletariat when it gets in the way of revolution. The faulty analyses which the ideologies of the Working Class have made, of the true nature of the Lumpen, are greatly responsible for the retardation of the development of the revolution in urban situtations. It can be said that the true revolutionaries in the urban centers of the world have been analyzed out of the revolution by some Marxist-Leninists.

Appendixes
The Ten-Point Program
Rules of the Black Panther Party

THE TEN-POINT PROGRAM

1. We Want Freedom. We Want Power To Determine
The Destiny Of Our Black Community.
We believe that Black people will not be free until we are
able to determine our destiny.

2. We Want Full Employment For Our People.
We believe that the federal government is responsible and
obligated to give every man employment or a guaranteed in-
come. We believe that if the White American businessmen
will not give full employment, then the means of production should be taken from the businessmen and placed in the
community so that the people of the community can organize and employ all of its people and give a high standard of
living.

3. We Want An End To The Robbery by The Capitalists
Of Our Black Community.
We believe that this racist government has robbed us, and
now we are demanding the overdue debt of forty acres and
two mules. Forty acres and two mules were promised 100
years ago as restitution for slave labor and mass murder of

Black people. We will accept the payment in currency which will be distributed to our many communities. The Germans are now aiding the Jews in Israel for the genocide of the Jewish people. The Germans murdered six million Jews. The American racist has taken part in the slaughter of over fifty million Black people; therefore, we feel that this is a modest demand that we make.

4. We Want Decent Housing Fit For The Shelter Of Human Beings.

We believe that if the White Landlords will not give decent housing to our Black community, then the housing and the land should be made into cooperatives so that our community, with government aid, can build and make decent housing for its people.

5. We Want Education For Our People That Exposes the True Nature Of This Decadent American Society. We Want Education That Teaches Us Our True History and Our Role In The Present-Day Society.

We believe in an educational system that will give to our people a knowledge of self. If a man does not have knowledge of himself and his position in society and the world, then he has little chance to relate to anything else.

6. We Want All Black Men To Be Exempt From Military Service.

We believe that Black people should not be forced to fight in the military service to defend a racist government that does not protect us. We will not fight and kill other people of color in the world who, like Black people, are being victimized by the White racist government of America. We will protect ourselves from the force and violence of the racist police and the racist military, by whatever means necessary.

7. We Want An Immediate End To Police Brutality And Murder Of Black People.

We believe we can end police brutality in our Black community by organizing Black self-defense groups that are dedicated to defending our Black community from racist police oppression and brutality. The Second Amendment to the Constitution of the United States gives a right to bear arms. We therefore believe that all Black people should arm themselves for self- defense.

8. We Want Freedom For All Black Men Held In Federal, State, County And City Prisons And Jails.

We believe that all Black people should be released from the many jails and prisons because they have not received a fair and impartial trial.

9. We Want All Black People When Brought To Trial To Be Tried In Court By A Jury Of Their Peer Group Or People From Their Black Communities, As Defined By The Constitution Of The United States.

We believe that the courts should follow the United States Constitution so that Black people will receive fair trials. The Fourteenth Amendment of the U.S. Constitution gives a man a right to be tried by his peer group. A peer is a person from a similar economic, social, religious, geographical, environmental, historical and racial background. To do this the court will be forced to select a jury from the Black community from which the Black defendant came. We have been, and are being, tried by all-White juries that have no understanding of the "average reasoning man" of the Black community.

10. We Want Land, Bread, Housing, Education, Clothing, Justice And Peace.

When, in the course of human events, it becomes necessary for one people to dissolve the political bands which have connected them with another, and to assume, among the powers of the earth, the separate and equal station to which the laws of nature and nature's God entitle them, a decent respect of the opinions of mankind requires that they should declare the causes which impel them to the separation.

We hold these truths to be self-evident, that all men are created equal; that they are endowed by their Creator with certain inalienable rights; that among these are life, liberty, and the pursuit of happiness. That, to secure these rights, governments are instituted among men, deriving their just powers from the consent of the governed; that, whenever any form of government becomes destructive of these ends, it is the right of the people to alter or abolish it, and to institute a new government, laying its foundation on such principles, and organizing its powers in such form, as to them shall seem most likely to effect their safety and happiness. Prudence, indeed, will dictate that governments long established should not be changed for light and transient causes; and, accordingly, all experience hath shown that mankind are more disposed to suffer, while evils are sufferable, than to right themselves by abolishing the forms to which they are accustomed. But, when a long train of abuses and usurpations, pursuing invariably the same object, evinces a design to reduce them under absolute despotism, it is their right, it is their duty, to throw off such government, and to provide new guards for their future security.

October 15, 1966

Rules of the Black Panther Party

Every member of the Black Panther Party throughout this country of racist America must abide by these rules as functional members of this party. Central Committee members, Central Staffs, and Local Staffs, including all captains subordinated to either national, state, and local leadership of the Black Panther Party will enforce these rules. Length of suspension or other disciplinary action necessary for violation of these rules will depend on national decisions by national, state or state area, and local committees and staffs where said rule or rules of the Black Panther Party were violated. Every member of the party must know these verbatim by heart. And apply them daily. Each member must report any violation of these rules to their leadership or they are counter-revolutionary and are also subjected to suspension by the Black Panther Party. The rules are:

1. No party member can have narcotics or weed in his possession while doing party work.
2. Any part member found shooting narcotics will be expelled from this party.

3. No party member can be drunk while doing daily party work.

4. No party member will violate rules relating to office work, general meetings of the Black Panther Party, and meetings of the Black Panther Party anywhere.

5. No party member will use, point, or fire a weapon of any kind unnecessarily or accidentally at anyone.

6. No party member can join any other army force, other than the Black Liberation Army.

7. No party member can have a weapon in his possession while drunk or loaded off narcotics or weed.

8. No party member will commit any crimes against other party members or black people at all, and cannot steal or take from the people, not even a needle or a piece of thread.

9. When arrested Black Panther members will give only name, address, and will sign nothing. Legal first aid must be understood by all Party members.

10. The Ten-Point Program and platform of the Black Panther Party must be known and understood by each Party member.

11. Party Communications must be National and Local.

12. The 10-10-10-program should be known by all members and also understood by all members.

13. All Finance officers will operate under the jurisdiction of the Ministry of Finance.

14. Each person will submit a report of daily work.

15. Each Sub-Section Leaders, Section Leaders, and Lieutenants, Captains must submit Daily reports of work.

16. All Panthers must learn to operate and service weapons correctly.

17. All Leaders who expel a member must submit this information to the Editor of the Newspaper, so that it will be published in the paper and will be known by all chapters and branches.

18. Political Education Classes are mandatory for general membership.

19. Only office personnel assigned to respective offices each day should be there. All others are to sell papers and do Political work out in the community, including Captain, Section Leaders, etc.

20. Communications- all chapters must submit weekly reports in writing to the National Headquarters.

21. All Branches must implement First Aid and/or Medical Cadres.

22. All Chapters, Branches, and components of the Black Panther Party must submit a monthly Financial Report to the Ministry of Finance, and also the Central Committee.

23. Everyone in a leadership position must read no less than two hours per day to keep abreast of the changing political situation.

24. No chapter or branch shall accept grants, poverty funds, money or any other aid from any government agency without contacting the National Headquarters.

25. All chapters must adhere to the policy and the ideology laid down by the Central Committee of the Black Panther Party.

26. All Branches must submit weekly reports in writing to their respective Chapters.

8 POINTS OF ATTENTION

1. Speak politely.
2. Pay fairly for what you buy.
3. Return everything you borrow.
4. Pay for anything you damage.
5. Do not hit or swear at people.
6. Do not damage property or crops of the poor, oppressed masses.
7. Do not take liberties with women.
8. If we ever have to take captives do not ill-treat them.

3 MAIN RULES OF DISCIPLINE

1. Obey orders in all your actions.
2. Do not take a single needle or piece of thread from the poor and oppressed masses.
3. Turn in everything captured from the attacking enemy.

www.ingramcontent.com/pod-product-compliance
Lightning Source LLC
Chambersburg PA
CBHW021617270326
41931CB00008B/736